A God for the Heart

*Discovering the Relational God
in the Story of the Prodigal Son*

Fred M. Taylor

Table of Contents

INTRODUCTION

The story of the Prodigal Son is one of the most well known stories that Jesus told. Many are familiar with its primary message, that being, the depravity of sin, the mercy of forgiveness, and the grace of redemption—or, to put it another way, rebellion, ruin, repentance, reconciliation, and restoration. The gospel in a nutshell.

But like other stories in the Scriptures, if one looks carefully one will not only find spiritual truth but insight into the often peculiar aspects of fallen, human nature. So, we not only come to know something of the nature of God but something about ourselves and who He created us to be in relation to Him. This is only one of the many beautiful aspects of this story.

Though the story is sometimes called a "parable," it seems, in my view, more like an actual situation which Jesus knew of and used as an illustrative teaching. Many understandably tend to focus on the waywardness of the prodigal son, but the story is really about a family that is not unlike many today, where beliefs and choices dramatically affect family dynamics. Thus, without the father and the older brother, the story would lack much of its impact. But taken together, all three can tell us much about God's love and the journey that we call our life (author Timothy Keller has suggested the story could be called "The Parable of the Two Lost Sons," while author, Henri Nouwen, sees another possible title in "The Parable of the Father's Love." Both, I think, provide fresh ways of viewing this drama).

Since Jesus was such a profound teacher and story teller, we can vividly imagine how things may have transpired. Though the story is simple and needs little interpretation, some elements and characters have been added to make it as relatable as possible to twenty-first century readers. I trust this will cause a deeper appreciation and a clearer understanding of the truths being taught. Additionally, because the imagery and drama provide such a rich setting, the in-bedded spiritual and psychological principles which run throughout are given special attention in short commentaries contained in the footnotes.

My use of the words, *Relational God*, may be curious to some, but I offer it as a way of emphasizing God's desire for relationship with us through Jesus Christ. And since "God *is* love" (I John 4:7-), how we relate to Him should ideally be based upon this central aspect of His Person, making the relationship an ever-growing interactive dynamic which can lead to genuine psychological and emotional wholeness and maturity.[1]

But to truly know the risen indwelling Christ, I believe three things are preferable. 1) A solid grounding in the eternal truths of Scripture. 2) A decision to enter into relationship with Christ. 3) A willing surrendering of our entire being to God. The first addresses the hunger in our mind for spiritual knowledge and understanding, while the last two speak to the relational and transformational needs of our deep heart respectively. We need not be "head-centered" at the expense of being "heart-centered," of vice-versa, for one compliments the other, and one cannot be truly appreciated without the other. And so, by engaging God in these ways, our mind is greatly challenged and our heart greatly expanded, wherein more of the eternal mysteries of God can become a reality in our lives.

Concerning those who obediently follow Him, Jesus said, "the kingdom of God is within you" (Luke 17:20-21). God's kingdom is not at all like any earthly kingdom, but rather one which, at this time in history, can only be entered into and known in an inward sense. For those who confess Jesus Christ as Savior and Master and possess His life and Spirit in their being, the Kingdom of God is a reality for them right now. As such, they are not looking for any earthly manifestation, for they already acknowledge Jesus' Kingship over their life. But, at

---

[1]Wholeness refers to something that is complete and sound in its entirety. According to Webster's, "whole" means being "in sound health; not diseased or injured; not broken, damaged, injured, defective, etc.; intact." The Greek word for "whole" is *holokleros*, which means "whole, having all of its parts, sound, perfect, complete in every part" (Mounce). Just as we were created in God's image (Gen.1:26), so we were meant to be a reflection of that image, for "men and women have the unique ability to image God to one another as well as to image God back up to God" (Mounce). Since Jesus is the full measure of the Godhead and we are complete in Him (Col.2:9-10), we were created to be whole and integrated people in every aspect of our being (I Thess.5:23). And because of the finished work of the cross of Christ, this will become reality one day, for God fully expects to see Himself in us as He designed us to be (Rom.8:18-29). In the meantime, as we continue growing in Him we are becoming what we are going to be in Christ.

the same time, they await His soon return in glory and the literal establishment of His Kingdom on this earth in the future.

For those of you who do not yet know Jesus as your Savior and Lord, my prayer is that you will. I also pray that you will discover how aggressively, intentionally, and unrelentingly He has been fighting for you, and that His intense desire for relationship truly makes Him *A God for the Heart.*

CHAPTER 1

Ego and Delusion

> A certain man had two sons. And the younger of them
> said to his father, "Father, give me the portion of goods
> that falls to me." So he divided to them his livelihood
> (Luke 15:11-12).

A cool breeze blew in from the west as the beautiful spring flora on the hillside slowly swayed with the gentle wind, bringing with it the fragrance of wild flowers from the hillside next to their home. Eliel caught their faint scent as he sat on a short, roughly-made four-legged stool next to the small wooden stall where their prized calf was kept. The calf was eating peacefully as he sat next to him.

He had just finished his chores and was now observing the usual morning activities—servants caring for the many sheep and goats and cows, tending the small orchard and vineyard, repairing broken structures. But Eliel was feeling anxious. He had made a decision and today was the day he would tell his father. The decision wasn't made in the spur-of-the-moment, but neither had he thought things through carefully or considered anything beyond his desire which, in truth, was his only real concern. And what *had* he decided? He wanted to leave home.

But why? Was he bored of the monotony of village life? Actually, he appreciated the structure, normalcy, and security that it provided along with the daily routines that went with it.

What about his living conditions? Was that a factor? Actually, compared to some who were just making a living from day to day, he enjoyed relative comfort. In fact, his father was well off enough to employ three servants to help with household matters and their property and livestock. So, Eliel never lacked for anything.

Had family relations become strained? Not really. Granted, he and his older brother Tobijah were not as close as they once were; their interactions of late characterized primarily by their brevity and superficiality, which both had become perfectly fine with over the last few years. But there had been no heated arguments or serious disagreements between them.

And when it came to his father...well, he wasn't the contentious type to start with; his most conspicuous traits being compassion and patience coupled with a plain spoken firmness. Eliel felt blessed to have such a father, for they spoke of the kind of man he was—kind, disciplined, and yet uncompromising when he needed to be.

So, in spite of the average things that often go on within families, everything was fine. And it was this which made him feel ambivalent at times about wanting to leave. It might not have been so puzzling to him if he were simply looking to strike out on his own, establish a name and reputation in his own right (which some in the community, no doubt, would have thought peculiar). But this was not about that.

Funny thing though, he never said a word to his father about what he was thinking or feeling. He knew he could talk to him; he was always able to talk with him about different things. But he really didn't want to. Actually, he wanted to avoid any discussion that might make him look as though he was rejecting all that was good in his life. Plus, he really didn't want to hear any well reasoned objections to his plans. For him, it wasn't any more complicated than just wanting the freedom to go and do as he pleased, to enjoy whatever pleasure life might have to offer in the moment.

Yet, by leaving he knew that he *would* be making it clear that he was no longer satisfied with his life as it was. Actually, part of him was...at least to a degree. But somewhere along the line he became persuaded that real fulfillment lay outside the confines of their small village, and that he could be much happier elsewhere. And now that sentiment had become a fixation in his *ego*.[2]

------

[2] *Ego* is the Greek word for the first personal pronoun "I." In Scripture, "the most significant usage of this pronoun is in the expressions of Jesus that begin with 'I am,' *ego eimi*" (Mounce). Examples of *ego eimi* can be found in the gospel of John (See John 6:35; 8:12; 10:7,9; 11:25; 14:6; 15:1). We sometimes view *ego* as arrogance, a self-exalted sense of oneself, or perhaps saving face, and it can certainly manifest in these ways. But "I" or "I am" essentially express what we think, what we want, how we feel, what we know, what we believe and, perhaps most importantly, how we see ourselves. Thus, psychologically, *ego* might best be understood as our present conscious awareness or our present point of view—in other words, how we currently see things. As such, *ego* tends to take the lead in most matters of life, for it seems to administrate the various other aspects and functions in our being. Consequently, what informs *ego* is most important. If we embrace God's truth and follow His light in our conscience, *ego* has the necessary foundation and illumination to be a channel for His love and grace. If,

Now of course, there was nothing at all wrong with wanting to be happy; it was how he was going about it that was problematic, for things had devolved into a very convoluted enterprise in his mind with respect to what being "happy" really meant to him. But if someone had asked him, he would have given them a good reason for wanting to leave. He *did* have reasons, mind you, but none of them would have been *the* reason. There *was* a pattern to his thinking despite the murkiness, but he just couldn't piece things together. Frankly, the thing that seemed most prevalent was simply a restlessness prodding him on, a desire for something different, something better, something else. And now, the obsession and fervor he felt in his soul were dragging him along like a pair of yoked oxen. He only knew one thing for certain: he didn't want to be *here* anymore, and that was good enough for now. The truth of the matter, however, lay beneath the surface of things, and that would remain concealed for the time being.[3]

And how long would his inheritance last? His father had taught him much about resource management, and he knew he needed to know such things; so a lot stuck with him. But these were never things he

---

however, we reject truth and light, deception and darkness become our lot, and we remain blind and alienated from God.

[3]Have we not all had similar thoughts at times? If only we could live in a certain place, have a particular thing, or be with a specific person, we would be happy. But the search for happiness can be elusive, often blinding us from seeing that what we desire may have little to do with our real needs. When telling this story, Jesus offered nothing directly on this issue, so nothing can be directly inferred, which begs the question: "Why even consider it since the primary emphasis is God's love and redemption?" (the story is really a continuation of the teaching Jesus began at the beginning of the chapter where He spoke of a man finding a lost sheep in the wilderness (Luke 15:3-7) and a woman finding a lost coin inside her house (Luke 15:8-10). Both of these teachings were meant to illustrate the pursuing nature of God's love for those who are lost. For if a man or woman are willing to search diligently for something that has no eternal value, how much more does God search out those whom He loves, whose value to Him greatly exceeds anything else in comparison?). But in order to grasp the story's profoundness, one thing is important to understand: God's dealings with fallen, sinful human nature. So the question is relevant, for it reflects a fundamental characteristic of human behavior, which is, none of us thinks, feels, believes, or does anything without a reason, even if it is unknown to us. And if our happiness is the goal, then we may be setting ourselves up for much hurt, for the desire to be happy can itself lead us into all sorts of quandaries due to the assumption that we often think we know what will make us happy, when all the while we are being driven by competing factions within us in an attempt to satisfy something in particular that we can't quite seem to put our finger on.

really wanted to know; his heart was usually elsewhere. Besides, some of those practical matters felt like additional clutter in his life. Yes, he knew at some point he would have to find work, and that what his father taught him would probably come in handy. But the work would have to support the lifestyle he wanted (which had yet to be clearly defined). This was most important to him.

Eliel was still sitting by the calf stall when something seemed to float upwards to his consciousness, piercing the peripheral chatter in his head. He loved his father, but he felt distant from him lately; the God of whom his father spoke so reverently and frequently seemed distant to him as well. Something seemed to be missing in both relationships, but he didn't know what. Was there some connection between the two? Did they have anything to do with his desire to leave? He didn't know that either, and he really wasn't all that disturbed enough to delve into the issues around them; just more clutter to sort through.

He started feeling somber as he sat there next to the stall. *Why am I feeling this now?* he thought. *I should be feeling excitement!* This was going to be a real adventure! He was starting a new life! He began to rally himself and think of all he was planning to do once he left—the places he would go, the sights he would see, the people he would meet.

Ah, there it is! The exhilaration he felt when the thought first came to him returned. Yes, this is what he needed to feel right now. Much better! But he couldn't completely shake that other feeling; reality had finally set in and it was sobering. *He was actually going to leave his family.*

He got up from the stool where he was sitting. The calf was still eating as he leaned over the railing and rubbed its head. "Goodbye, Mushi!" It was time to tell his father.

He began walking towards the house, rehearsing in his mind how he would say things. This could be touchy. According to Jewish custom, he knew he had a right to a share of his father's estate. But by asking for his inheritance *before* his father's death, he was about to take things to a whole new level. He really didn't know how his father would respond.[4]

He knew his older brother would be appalled. He could hear him now. *He* would never do such a thing! Tobijah had his faults for sure, but when it came to family, he embodied all the characteristics you would expect from one who was next in line to become the patriarchal head. But Eliel never felt much jealousy over Tobijah being the first-born; he never really wanted the responsibility that came with it.

His heart was pounding when he stepped into the room where their two oxen were kept, continuing through the courtyard and towards his father's study. It was quiet around the house. Tobijah was out doing other things. That was good; he didn't want him around right now. He walked in and found his father standing behind his desk looking over some things. Tall, with salt and pepper hair and beard, he was a strong man, stalwart in attitude and conduct. His integrity, humility, and calm, soft-spoken manner were well known in the village; everyone looked up to him with respect and honor.

Eliel immediately felt intimidated, and now he had trouble remembering the words he had just rehearsed. For a culture that stressed strict obedience to fathers, he knew his request could not only be considered dishonorable and contemptuous, but warrant a beating; his father was well within his rights to do so by Jewish custom. Then a thought occurred to him: *What if he kicks me out of the house and demand that I make my own way in life? What if he legally disinherits me? I would have nothing!* He suddenly realized that he might be taking a bigger risk than he thought!

His father looked up at him when he entered the room. For a moment, both just stared at one another, each waiting for the other to say something. The father had known that something was off about Eliel

---

[4]Imagine your son asking you what you plan to leave him after you die, and then demand that you give it to him now! This could easily come across as, "I wish you were already dead!" Now let's add injury to insult. Most, if not all, of the father's wealth was probably in property holdings and livestock. According to Jewish custom, he could decide which assets or pieces of property would go to which sons after his death. Until then, he was the manager and received all the profits. Therefore, he was under no obligation to give his son anything at this point. So, to give him the "portion of goods" meant he had to liquidate some of his land holdings or livestock, which would substantially decrease his assets.

for a few days; he hadn't been acting himself lately. He had planned to ask him about it today, but now here he was, obviously wanting to say something.

"What is it, son?" he asked.

"Father, I've thought about it and...I want to leave home, see other places, experience new things." He thought he should qualify his statement. "It's not that I don't like it here anymore, but...well, I just want a different...I mean, I want to start a new life for myself. So, I want the portion of goods that are mine by inheritance!"

Even Eliel cringed a little when he finally heard the words come out of his mouth. In his head, they sounded more rational, but now that they had been spoken, he heard the entitlement, the insensitivity, the arrogance! A twinge of guilt came on him, not enough, though, to dissuade him, but just enough to feel the prick in his conscience. But it was to late to take the words back.[5]

The look in his father's eyes was stern, penetrating—as if he were looking right through him. He was thinking what could have prompted this; and then it made sense. *So, this is the reason for his behavior!* His expression changed, as though a club had just been hammered into his chest. He knew his son had no understanding of what he was asking, nor how leaving in such a way might bring certain consequences in the future. He wondered if all of the time and effort poured into the boy over the years had been in vain, or worse, rejected because of some childish, impulsive urge.

---

[5]The Greek word for conscience, *syneidesis*, literally means "a knowing with" or "a co-knowledge (with oneself) (Vine's). Conscience is "that part of the mind that performs moral judgments and ethical evaluations" regarding our actions and attitudes (Mounce). Since the basis for conscience is the moral law of God which has been written on the heart of every person (Rom.2:15), conscience is part of our innate design as beings created in the image of God. So, like the apostle Paul, we should strive "to keep [our] conscience clear before God and man" (Acts 24:16) by obeying what we know to be true. By doing so we can possess a "good" conscience (I Tim.1:5) or a "pure" conscience (II Tim.1:3) that "testifies" to what is right with "simplicity and godly sincerity" (II Cor.1:12). Paul lived in "good conscience before God" (Acts 23:1) because he believed he was doing God's will when he followed his conscience. Notwithstanding, conscience can be corrupted. By not living according to what we know to be true, our conscience can become "seared" (scorched, hardened), such as when a hot iron cauterizes the skin and it becomes callous and unresponsive to feeling (I Tim.4:2); "defiled," depraved, morally bad, perverted (Titus 1:15); or even "evil," wicked (Heb.10:19-22).

Eliel was fidgeting now, nervously looking around at things, then looking back at his father who had yet to say anything. He was feeling even more self-conscious. *Say something, please!* he thought.

And then it hit him. He wasn't just leaving his family, he was making an unequivocal statement to his father: "I will be fine without you!" His relationship with him, as he knew it, was over! Naively, a part of him thought his father would always be in his life in some way, certainly not as he was now but to some degree at least—perhaps an occasional visit here and there. But now he realized that things would *never* be the same again between them after today.[6]

His father was about to reply with a hard "No," and a reasoned, though undeserved, explanation as to why. Then he heard words deep inside: *"Give it to him and let him go!"* He wasn't expecting that, but the words were unambiguous. This clearly went against what would otherwise be prudent! But he knew from Whom the words came, and knowledge and experience had taught him to always obey. He stood there for a moment, considering the implications. He was troubled, and Eliel could see it. Intuitively, he knew this had little to do with his son wanting a "new life," at least not as the boy might have envisioned it.

"I will make the arrangements." And that was all he said. He dropped what he was doing and walked out of the house towards the village square.

---

[6]When all is said and done, it's not so much our accomplishments, wealth, fame, or status which provide meaning and fulfillment but the close relationships which nurtured our soul and made us feel known, accepted, and loved. And the central relationship is with Christ. Thus, we constantly seek out those things which find their origin in Him while often remaining completely unaware of this fact. Every issue we face in life can be traced back to relational issues with God. We cannot escape this reality, even if we refuse to believe He even exists. In fact, that assertion alone often contradicts what really drives us, for the spiritual imperative implanted by God within us to return to Him as our Source is the most foundational aspect of our being. Indeed, everything in life goes back to the reality that God is the Creator of all things and all things derive their existence and being from Him (Col.1:16-17). And it's precisely because of this that we encounter a myriad of emotions when it comes to God, for the one relationship that provides the joy, security, peace, meaning, love, and purpose we seek in life is also the most mysterious and, at times, the most perplexing, frustrating, and unpredictable of all. Therefore, faith, humility, and an adventurous heart are prerequisites if we wish to have an *authentic* relationship with the living God.

The square was large and made a nice gathering place for the one hundred and fifty or so people who lived in the village. Large trees provided shade for several benches which had been made; a few people were relaxing and conversing on them while other people were going about their daily business at the market. Shop owners were busy—the blacksmith was fitting shoes for a horse, a man was squabbling with the shoemaker over the price of repairing some sandals, the weaver was making baskets, the potter was sculpting a vase on his wheel. Two women were drawing water from the communal well. They smiled and addressed the father reverently as he walked by, giving him honor as one of the chief elders in the village. He smiled but kept walking, having not said a word to them or anyone in the square.

He had walked the length of the village and was now alone, standing just outside its boundaries and looking at the immense fields of wheat and barley which would soon be harvested by him and others in the village who owned the lands. He thought about the rhythmic cycle of seed time and harvest, of the earth itself, and how it often sharply contrasted with the seeming unpredictability of human nature, especially when it came to family. He looked up to heaven. "Lord, You know exactly what You're doing, and I trust You!"

Eliel was still standing in the house, trying to interpret the meaning of his father's short response. Part of him felt a little indignant that his petition was granted so quickly; it caught him off guard. He was expecting something more—a short lecture, an inquiry into his motives, an attempt to reason with him. He got none of those. Granted, he really didn't want to hear anything that would have challenged him. It wouldn't have mattered anyway; he wasn't in a place emotionally or mentally to even hear what his father might have said. But he wondered, *Is he so offended that he no longer wants me around?* It frightened him.

That evening, Eliel was caring for their two oxen. He had just given them provender and was brushing them down. During the day, his brother Tobijah had said nothing to him. Over the last few years, things had been steadily deteriorating between them, and now this matter only added to the growing mutual indifference. When they were younger, Tobijah was his hero, protecting him when other kids were being unusually nasty. He could depend on him. But that was then. Now, having grown up and become two very different people, they might have appeared unrelated to an outsider.

Tobijah walked in. He was as tall as their father, and built solid; years of strenuous labor had toned every inch of his muscular body. Easily the more ambitious one of the two, he was always ready to step up, do what was necessary, tackle difficult things; a natural leader.

And good looking, too! Some of the young women in the village would talk giddily among themselves about him. Indeed, his curly black hair, trimmed beard, and strong rugged masculine features easily conjured up images of how Israel's heroes and warriors of the past may have looked. In comparison, Eliel was shorter, lanky, clean shaven, and not nearly as good-looking—at least not in his mind.

Tobijah wasted no time. With the meticulous precision of a scribe analyzing and interpreting the Torah, he began berating Eliel, picking him apart piece by piece for his selfishness, his irrationality, his immaturity.[7]

On and on it went, his voice becoming louder and louder. Eliel tried to counter him on some things but he really couldn't disagree with much of what he was saying; he'd had some of the same thoughts and couldn't sort through them. And now, feeling rebuked, he felt like the same dumb little brother who still didn't know what he was doing with his life.

When it seemed Tobijah would never stop, he finally did, apparently exhausted after his verbal bombardment. Then he asked the one simple question Eliel still couldn't answer for himself.

"Why are you doing this? And why just before harvest?"

"I don't expect you to understand," Eliel said, not bothering to even look at him as he continued brushing down the ox.

---

[7]Scribes were teachers of Mosaic Law, the Torah (Heb. *tora*-instruction, guidance, law), which not only consisted of the five books of Moses known as the Pentateuch (Genesis, Exodus, Leviticus, Numbers, and Deuteronomy) but the entire body of Jewish literature.

"Then *help* me to understand! What is your purpose in doing this? All father said was that you want to start a 'new life!' What does that mean? Doing what, exactly?"

His questions only underscored how far apart they had drifted over the years. Eliel was not about to bare his soul in such a hostile atmosphere, especially about something that required a lot more context and a good amount of patience to understand what was hard to explain. Tobijah never had much appreciation for nuance, especially when it came to matters of the heart; he needed things in black and white.

Eliel looked at him. "You've never wanted anything more than what you have now."

"I've never *needed* anything more than what I have now! Tell me, what do you want that you don't already have?"

Eliel became angry. "Since when do you care about what I want? You and I haven't had a real conversation in years, and the last time we talked, you didn't understand...no, no, you didn't even *try* to understand how I saw things!"

"That's because you're ungrateful...always have been! You've never really appreciated what you had! Why would I waste time trying to 'understand' you when you apparently disdain the very things and people which have made your life what it is?"

That hurt more than Eliel let on. He looked down for a moment. There was no use. Obviously, his brother had decided long ago who he was, and there was nothing he could say to change that. His brother had no interest in trying to "understand" him; he already thought he did. Eliel went back to brushing the ox.

Tobijah assumed their "talk" was over, and began to walk out of the room. Reaching the doorway, he turned and said rather calmly, "Did you ever once think about how this would affect father? He will probably never be seen the same way again in this community!" He walked out.

That got Eliel's attention. He hadn't thought about that, nor about how getting his inheritance would change his father's financial condition—reason being, he just wanted what he wanted, and the thought of how his choices might impact others or that he should be held responsible for his choices was never a consideration. It was as simple as that.

But, truth be told, Tobijah was angrier with their father than with his brother; he couldn't understand why he did this for Eliel. Their father had spent a lifetime working hard, increasing their possessions and living in integrity, and now their assets would be diminished and the family's honor tarnished, perhaps to the next generation.

As the firstborn, he wondered how all of this would affect him when the time came. Needing to rebuild financially was a given, but would he also have to restore the family name? He knew his brother could be thoughtless at times, but his father's reaction was inexcusable. There was only one explanation in his mind that made any sense to him: *Just as Joseph was Jacob's favorite, so Eliel is to father!*

The next day, word quickly spread through the village that the boy was leaving and that his father was selling off a portion of his holdings and livestock. Everyone was in absolute shock when they heard the reason why. Most could not understand why he would do such a thing for his son; it was not only wrong but seemed out of character for him. One of the other village elders took the opportunity to lecture him, reminding him of his position in the community and the example he was setting by his actions. Another elder went so far as to boldly declare, "This man is weak when it really counts!"[8]

---

[8]The father was not only the provider of the family, but the source of its identity. The family was known in the community by the father's name, character, and reputation. Therefore, given the patriarchal traditions of the day, most of the people listening to Jesus tell this story were probably aghast, wondering why this father would abdicate his role as the leader of his family and do such a thing. Unlike the father in this story, we sometimes see fathers who walk away from their responsibilities, causing many to dismiss them altogether, seeing them as unloving, incompetent, or irrelevant; the very word "father" itself has a negative connotation in the minds of many. But the symbolism in this story is meant to point us to God, the Perfect Father (Heb.12:9), for He is the One from whom every earthly father should draw understanding as to what being a father really means. However, before a man can become the kind of father that his family needs, he must first come to know and experience deeply the love that God the Father has for *him*. He must not only allow God to *"father him"* in every area of his life but accept *how* God chooses to father him. This is especially critical during times of testing, discipline, and hardship, for it is often during these times that we are tempted to in-

But little by little the people came over the next few days, carting off newly acquired items and livestock. Most in the community chose not to buy anything, but everyone it seemed had an opinion about what was happening.

Nathan, the father's dearest friend who lived on the opposite side of the village, came as well. He didn't want to buy anything, but he was very curious as to what might have happened for Eliel to want to take off like this; what was *really* going on with the boy? Nathan had a son, too, but also a daughter, and he sometimes noticed how she and Eliel would exchange glances whenever they saw one another; nothing overtly flirtatious, but Nathan saw that they were obviously interested in one another. But now that the boy was leaving, both Nathan and his daughter were confused.

But the father wasn't the only one who felt the rebuke of the village leaders; Eliel did as well. Part of him cared because they were his elders. Having known him for all of his life, Eliel respected them, knowing they meant well. But aside from them, he wasn't all that concerned with what others thought. And for those few who were the village busybodies and gossipers who could always be counted upon to inflame and embellish things, he had even less regard. Eliel had heard his share of dramas concerning others over the years, and now he knew he was the major character in the latest one.

But those few days were stressful, for until things were sold he couldn't leave, and the waiting time proved harder for him than he expected. The tension in the house between he and Tobijah was palpable even though little was said between them. They were strangers now, neither one feeling as if they knew the other.

But when a third of everything had finally been sold, the father asked Eliel to come to his study. He was intensely sad that things had

terpret things as evidence of God being uninvolved, harsh, or absent—just as our earthly fathers may have been. But everything God does in our life is to bring us into maturity so that we become a reflection of who He is. Consequently, God's approach to fathering is most certainly "hands on." And this is exactly how He would be, for if evil men are able to manifest the nature and characteristics of their spiritual father (John 8:41-44), how much more should followers of Christ manifest the nature and characteristics of *their* spiritual Father?

to be this way, but confident that, even in the midst of so much confusion and obstinacy, God was mysteriously at work. Whatever God's purpose was in this, it *would* be realized.

"Here is your portion, son," the father said. Eliel held his hands out. As soon as the coins touched them he felt a surge of emotion come over him, as if a great power had now become his. His father saw it and made a note, for it said much to him concerning his son's perspective with regard to material things.

"Thank you, father," is all Eliel said. Immediately, he went to his room, laid the coins on his bed, and looked at them. Real autonomy was now his! He wanted to make them last as long as possible—at least that was the plan. He stashed the coins in a small pouch, placing them at the bottom of his large sack. Then he began gathering what little he thought he would need and placing them in the sack.

But he was having trouble concentrating. During the last few days, there were fleeting moments when it felt as if another person was present in him, a person he somehow recognized but didn't fully know, who brought dark, disturbing thoughts and feelings with him that Eliel had worked hard to forget. Eliel didn't like this person or the troubling things he brought. But here he was and here they were, threatening to bring his kingdom, which he had been painstakingly building to the glory of self for years, to ruins.[9]

---

[9]Some have seen a little of the darkness within them, while others have seen a great deal; some are in denial about it, while others accept it; some find it upsetting, while others gain some understanding of themselves; some fight it fiercely, while others embrace it. But irrespective of how we see it, until these pockets of darkness are transformed by God's power, they remain in us and part of who we are. These dark contents are things we have consciously rejected, ignored, downplayed, hidden, justified, projected, repressed, or attempted to control because they conflict with how we see ourselves or want to be seen. These are things which cause anger, shame, revulsion, uneasiness, resentment, fear, grief, desire, confusion, or any number of such things, for they have never been properly addressed and dealt with (and it's not just the things we might consider negative, but things that are actually benign which others may have rejected, and we in turn did the same). Sometimes we are unaware of their existence and energy, but they can reveal themselves at the most inopportune times—such as, when we are pushed to the extreme, or react to something impulsively, or by accidental slips of the tongue, or incidental displays in our behavior. Whether we are consciously aware of them or not, their influence remains, but if we choose to "put off, concerning [our] former conduct, the old man" and "put on the new man which was created according to God, in true righteousness and holiness" (Eph.4:22,24), and "walk as children of light"

But how could he admit there might be something wrong on the inside? He couldn't. That would betray the false beliefs to which he was now dedicated, and that could mean having to face some hard things, which might lead to the dreadful conclusion that he was indeed deluded! *That* was not an option![10]

Eliel was no longer packing things but standing there, as if in a trance. When he came to, he immediately pushed the thoughts away and reminded himself that this *was* what he really wanted. But it was too late. His decision had already set things in motion, and his father's prayers for him had already been heard and received. There was no going back now. He was on a collision course with Reality.

It was afternoon when Eliel finally walked out of the house. Two servants watched him as they were cleaning things. There were no goodbyes between them, and that was just as well. They were still confused as to why the boy was, in their view, seemingly throwing ev-

---

(Eph.5:8) according to Christ's life within us, we give the Holy Spirit opportunity to begin transforming the darkness. Indeed, if we truly "walk in the light as He (Jesus) is in the light" (I John 1:7) it will *expose* the darkness. Thus, when we muster the courage to face ourselves, the power of God's redemptive love is available to transform these dark places and make them a part of our strength instead of our shame.

[10]Our false sense of reality—the fertile breeding ground for delusional thinking—is the basis for our false self, our "mistaken identity." The false self, which arises from and is sustained by the wounded places in our heart, becomes our plan for self-redemption apart from God, our defense against further pain. And this false self gives rise to *personas*. To the Pharisees, Jesus once said, "inside you are full of hypocrisy" (Matt.23:28). The Greek word for hypocrite is *hypokrites*, which originally referred to actors who used masks to augment the force of their voice in dialogue. It "was later applied to someone who acted in real life or who pretended to be something that he was not, especially in the moral aspects of life" (Mounce). Just as physical masks hide our true facial expressions, our words and behavior can hide our true inner state, so much so that people often meet the "person as presented as opposed to the person as real." There does, however, seem to be a slight distinction. While *personas* are often adopted for purposes of social expectations, personal gain, and appearance, hypocrisy is inherently deceptive and reveals an arrogance rooted in the lies we steadfastly continue to believe. We have become unwilling to hear and accept anything which contradicts our present point of view. One who has adopted a *persona* can often admit they have done so—that is, if they have not completely identified with it to the point of losing sight of what is true. But the hypocrite can admit to no such thing. It's as though an extreme degree of self-centered blindness coupled with a contempt for truth has made humility nearly impossible. It should go without saying that any attempt to relate to God through such disingenuous means will be met with resistance. We will get nowhere with Him if a self-righteous hypocrisy has become our *modus operandi*.

erything, including his life, away. They could never even dream of having a life like his. One of them looked at the boy with disdain. He couldn't believe how one so privileged could be so ungrateful.

Eliel didn't expect to see Tobijah, but he had just left the sheep enclosure and was coming around the side of the house when he saw Eliel leaving; he stopped and watched as Eliel walked towards the village square. Tobijah wasn't sure what he was feeling in that moment aside from a slight sense of detachment. His brother was leaving and that was that.

Walking through the square, Eliel saw a few people looking at him. There were plenty of people in the square but no one said anything to him; shop keepers kept on working. Two men were talking with one another as they looked at the boy, and then turned their backs. A few little kids with whom Eliel would chase and hold and tickle on occasion smiled and waved at him; one ran up to him a hugged him. Other than that, everyone continued going about their business.

Their village was situated on a slightly elevated hilltop overlooking a valley where the fertile fields grew. There was a path, about a hundred yards long and wide enough for carts, that led down the hillside to the main road towards the nearby town that was about two miles away. Everyone had to take this path if they were going to that town.

When Eliel finally got to the edge of their village where the path began, he saw Rapha, one of his father's servants with whom he had developed an unexpected friendship over the years, waiting for him. Eliel hadn't told Rapha very much about his plans and Rapha wondered why. Was it because he was just a "servant?" He didn't think that was the reason since they had talked about personal issues before. But Rapha thought there might be something more about this situation that caused Eliel to be less candid than normal. Whatever the reason, Rapha thought it best to not press the issue.

Eliel stopped in front of Him.

"Well...I guess this is goodbye,"Eliel said, "at least for now. I'm sure we'll see each other again."

Rapha had a sad face. "Where will you go?"

"I'm going north, and then I'll see where that leads me."

Rapha knew Eliel was being purposely vague, but he really didn't need to know specifics. He tried to lighten the moment. "You know you're leaving me at the mercy of your brother, don't you? Who can I play the trickster with now?"

"Just think of it this way. With me gone, you'll have to be far more creative if you want him to play along!"

"You mean I'll have to be far more careful! I'm not even sure if Tobijah still remembers how to smile, much less laugh!" They both laughed. Then Rapha grabbed Eliel and hugged him. After their embrace, Rapha looked at him. "You know that your father has been a father to me as well—in many ways. So, I know this must be hard for him. But it seems you must do this." With a very serious look of his face, Rapha said, "I hope you find what you're looking for!"

Eliel was struck by the statement. He took it as an insinuation of something infantile in him. *Am I not old enough to know what I want in life?* Of course, Rapha didn't mean it that way.

Eliel started down the path and saw his father standing on the main road. When Eliel reached him, his father, without saying a word, gave him a long hug and then a kiss on each cheek. Eliel felt a deep love emanating from him, but it felt strangely devoid of emotion—like a detached compassion that was both reassuring and disturbing at the same time.

"Goodbye, father." Eliel didn't know what else to say in that moment, so he started down the road. He turned and took one last look at his father; he was still standing in the same place, watching. He waved but his father didn't wave back. Eliel thought if things turned out the way he was hoping, he would not see him or the village again for a very long time.

As he got further away from the village, he expected to see more people on the road, but there were only a few. This particular road was usually safe to travel, more so than the more remote roads where there were few towns and villages between them. On those roads, Eliel knew it was best to travel with a small group or part of a caravan; robbers were known to prey upon people on those roads. Roman built stone paved roads were the safest of all because of the high foot traffic. The military transported troops and supplies throughout the empire on their roads, and merchants used them to bring goods to various cities. Eliel knew he would eventually have to travel on one of them to get to where he was going.

And just where *was* he going?...to a city he heard about through a merchant whom he and his father happened upon one day in the town near their village. The man was well traveled, having seen and experienced many things, and the way he talked about this particular country and its people made it seem especially exciting and exotic. Eliel was so fascinated that he never forgot it.

But it wasn't just the country that excited him. Sometimes, thoughts of who *he* was apart from his upbringing came to his mind. They were curiously enticing, but he felt conflicted at times for just having them, as though the thoughts themselves were a betrayal of his culture. But now that he had the opportunity to explore them, he was feeling enthusiastic; he saw this an opportunity to become more than who he was. *Maybe a new environment is what I need to find a new me!* That thought felt freeing in itself![11]

---

[11]God, for His part, has already done what was needed for us to become all that we were created to be, for through "His divine power [He] has given to us all things that pertain to life and godliness, through the knowledge of Him who called us by glory and virtue," having given us "exceeding great and precious promises, that through these [we] may be partakers of the divine nature" (II Pet.1:3-4). The first key for this to become a reality in our life is understanding that it is only *in Christ* that we find our *true* self, the person we were designed by God to be (Eph.1:3-5), for as the apostle Paul said, "in *Him* we live, and move, and have our being" (Acts 17:28, italics added). The second key is realizing that our journey is not so much striving towards some notion of individuality or self-expression as much as it is discovering God's intention for us from the foundation of the world. This is important, for how often do we reject the innate patterns of the heart as beings created in God's image in favor of something which caters to our *ego*, only to find that we are striving against that which is actually natural for us? The third key is the most demanding and mysterious, which is, being unwilling to settle for anything less than what God desires or us. Granted, there are some things which will not become a reality for us in this lifetime and will only be fulfilled when we are finally and fully manifested as the sons and daughters of God (Rom.8:18-25). But much of what God desires for us can be experienced now. So, even in our waywardness, God makes use of everything at His disposal in order that we might be who we were meant to be. Thus, God never abandons us or becomes indifferent to our plight or complicit with our disobedience. He simply understands what needs to take place for us to come into spiritual maturity. So, no matter what choices we make, the decision as to how our choices will fulfill God's will for our life has already been made, for He is

Dust flew around his sandals; his gait was brisk. He had a very long trip ahead of him and he wanted to be at a certain wayside inn before nightfall—rest overnight, then head out again the next morning. He was munching on a fig he had taken from his sack when Rapha's words came back to him. He thought about it. If he *was* looking for something, he was confident that he would find it where he was going, and he would know it when he found it.

---

light years ahead of us and will always have the final say. Nevertheless, though we have the freedom to choose, God sees to it that, should we still decide to reject Him or His plan for our life, our choice reflects a decision of our will and not a lack of understanding and opportunity. In other words, we reject Him with the *knowledge* that we are rejecting Him.

CHAPTER 2

Enter the Far Country

> And not many days after, the younger son gathered all together, journeyed to a far country, and there wasted his possessions with prodigal living. But when he had spent all, there arose a severe famine in that land, and he began to be in want (Luke 15:13-14).

The terrain was mostly desert; formidable and unforgiving. Eliel had entered the country that morning. It was now afternoon and he was still walking! How much further would it be? In the distance he could see what looked like figures moving eastward. Or maybe it was a mirage. It was hard to tell; waves of heat continued to rise from the ground. But it wasn't a mirage. He saw a caravan, and it had to be taking the major route that led to the city. When he finally got to it, he felt invigorated; this was indeed the road, and the city was near. He would soon be at his destination.

Upon arriving he felt a little overwhelmed by how big the city actually was; like a huge, sprawling metropolis—much larger than the small towns and villages that were scattered throughout his home country. The city had so many attractions and diversions that he thought he might be swept away by its immensity. But once he became familiar with the many streets and knew where everything was, he began moving about with just as much ease and confidence as the locals.

Being a commercial trading center and military outpost for the Romans, the city was entirely centered around the main street which ran through the middle of it. The street was bordered by stone colonnades, each commanding attention for their impressive crafting and sculpture. As he walked down the street, there were many caravans carrying goods as they passed one another along the route; and lots of people, more than he had ever seen in his life, going in every direction! Away from the main thoroughfare there were many large and beautiful buildings—some looking governmental and administrative while others seemed for other purposes—each showcasing the architectural flavor of the city.

Right away, Eliel had a sense about the place. There was a permissiveness about it, as though one could do almost anything they wanted. And like himself, he saw many foreigners who seemed at ease milling about in this very accommodating culture. Seeing this made him feel even more comfortable. *Here*, he thought, *is where I can be myself!* The city seemed a perfect fit to him, and it wouldn't take long before he felt like he belonged.

On his first day he spent time walking around and observing things. Everything had his attention—the sights, the sounds, the smells. Things were so strange, a little intimidating as well, but pretty close to how he had imagined them based upon what he had heard. Other things were nothing like he thought they would be, completely alien to him. Either way, he thought the Gentiles here had a *very* interesting culture!

Like most large cities, there was a bustling marketplace that sold just about everything one could need—food, perfumes, supplies, spices, tools, fabrics, animals, ointments, etc. Most of the items for sale were from the local people, but some had obviously come from other places, brought in by traveling merchants. The majority of the buyers looked to be regular town folk going about their daily routines, purchasing what they needed as they haggled with sellers over prices. But foreigners were also there, creating a cosmopolitan atmosphere. All the while, donkeys brayed loudly, horses pulled carts full of produce and materials through the hordes of people, chickens squawked in their wooden cages, sellers yelled as they advertised their wares, and children ran around playing and screaming unsupervised. The place was as noisy as one would expect.

At various places in the city, he noticed temples and altars dedicated to various gods—some to well known Roman gods and others to gods indigenous to the region. Eliel had heard how some cities were so completely enmeshed in religion that it dominated every aspect of life, both public and private. This city seemed to be no exception; you couldn't miss the fact that certain deities obviously held very important places in the lives of many. Each god, it seemed, demanded certain things, and the people were more than willing to acquiesce in order to obtain their favors. Eliel thought how strange some of their practices were as they sought to appease and petitioned their gods.

He came upon one particular temple which stood out from the rest. It was a very large building with an equally large open air court before it. Connected to an arch, it was surrounded by porticoes and raised upon carefully cut masonry; an altar lay just inside of its entrance beyond a short flight of stone stairs. Standing a good distance from it, he watched people performing devotions at the altar—lighting candles, praying, and chanting to the god it honored—while others went in and out of the temple. He could smell the putrid odor of offerings being made as well as sweet smelling incense being burned.

After leaving the temple, weariness from his long journey began to set in; he started looking for lodging. A place caught his eye. It looked as if it catered to well-to-do travelers, so he thought it would be suitable for the time he would be here. Making his way through the crowds, he headed towards it. It was a large two-storied quadrangular shaped building with an inner courtyard where horses and camels belonging to the guests were kept and cared for. Travelers stayed in one of the many rooms on the second floor.

As he got closer, the innkeeper, a short, stout man who was well-dressed, just happened to be standing outside and saw Eliel coming his way. The man knew immediately that Eliel was not a local, as his clothes indicated he was foreign and most likely from a family that was relatively well off; the common folk he was used to seeing around town usually never wore such clothing. He spoke first.

"So, where are *you* from my friend? Are you looking for a room?" Eliel was hoping to be more inconspicuous so as not to stand out, but it seemed that would be impossible.

"I'm from a region south of here...and yes, I do need a room. Are you the owner?"

"I'm the manager. But tell me, what country are you from?" The man learned much about the world through the many travelers who stayed at the inn, and he liked to tell his friends about where they were all from and the interesting stories they shared. But Eliel was hesitant; it might lead to other questions that he really didn't want to answer.

"The Roman province of Judea," he finally replied.

He could see the boy wasn't a merchant, nor did he seem to be passing through. "Yes, I know of that area. So, why have you come to our country?"

"I'm starting a new life!"

So, what was wrong with the old life? the man thought. *Better not be too nosy. I need the money!*

"If you've come to get away from the Romans, as you can see they are here, too. We're at the boundary of their empire. Further east are where the *real* barbarians live. And there's no protection there!" Eliel had noticed a military presence in the city who were obviously there to maintain the *Pax Romana*. The local authorities, however, seemed to be the primary law enforcers.

"No, I wanted to come to this city because of the many things I've heard that one can do here. Am I right or were the stories I've been told simply exaggerations?"

"Oh no, you're quite right! There are many things to do here! Tell me what you like and I will help you find it."

"I like many things. I just want to have a good time and have fun."

"Fun costs money, my friend."

Eliel carefully pulled out his small pouch, reached in, and showed him a few coins. "As you can see, I have money."

The man looked at them and smiled. "Well then, for a small fee, on top of the price of lodging of course, I know some things that might interest you. Come inside and see the rooms. You can pick the one you like, and then I will tell you where you might find some "fun."

What was a small fee if the man could give him the "lay of the land;" Eliel knew he could afford it. Besides, he liked the way the man said it, as though he was especially knowledgeable about this sort of thing. Maybe he would even tell him about things that most travelers never see.

With his sack slung over his shoulder containing his pouch of coins, provisions, cooking utensils, and his sleeping mat tucked under one arm, he followed the man inside and up to the second floor. This establishment was far more accommodating and comfortable than the rock-enclosed rooms at the wayside inns where pack animals also slept and vermin frequented. Sleeping on a wooden floor tonight would be a welcome relief from the dirt. Plus, the security of a safer environment made him feel like a valued guest. He was feeling good about his choice to come here, and was looking forward to enjoying everything the city had to offer. He purposes to not deny himself any pleasure; *nothing* would be off limits.

Little did he know that his stay in the country would be the most difficult time of his life, for he had just entered school—the "School in the Far Country," and some very harsh lessons awaited him, courtesy of God and two of His most reliable instructional aides: pain and suffering. As things would have it, natural conditions would force him to adapt to his surroundings for his physical survival, and spiritual conditions would force him to engage with inner realities for his spiritual well-being. And both would demand that he do so on *their* terms.[12]

---

[12]One unfortunate reality regarding spiritual life is that we can hear and agree with truth but never really learn the vital lessons in an inward way. To put it another way, we can acknowledge truth with our words, mentally assent to its importance with our intellect, but not truly live our life according to it, much less be in submission to He who *is* Truth. There are several reasons for this. We may sequester truth in our head, preventing it from entering our heart where genuine transformation occurs; we may equate an intellectual understanding of truth with actually possessing it spiritually; we may see truth as relative and *our* truth as sufficient or just as valid as any other; we may be afraid that truth will change our life as we know it while revealing every ugly thing in us; or we may be in rebellion against truth because it opposes our *ego*-centered way of life. Therefore, pain often becomes necessary. Now the fact that we must experience pain in order to learn certain things is an absolute affront to our *ego*, but it seems that when all else fails to get our attention on a heart level, pain has a way of doing just that. Pain can come in many forms—difficult circumstances, unfulfilled desires, heartbreaking loss, sickness or disease, tragic news, etc. Whatever it may be, God may use it to ambush those of us who are focused on other things or steadfastly resistant to His will, for pain touches us at our very core. And when God does finally have our complete and undivided attention, we can get a glimpse of eternal things—that is, if we are willing to see beyond the pain and not become resentful because of it. Therefore, the real issue is not pain at all, but whether or not we are willing to trust God in spite of it and learn what He is trying to teach us in the midst of it (and this is often a challenge itself, for what we *think* we need to learn may not at all be what God is trying to teach us). In-

Unbeknownst to Eliel, the "fun" would be short-lived.

The bounty of wheat was expected to be very generous this year. The father was surveying his land as he thought about how many hired servants he wanted for this year's harvest. Tobijah looked over their vast acreage and offered a number that he thought would be sufficient; his father nodded in agreement. Then, as he often did everyday, he looked towards the road leading to town. Tobijah knew why.

"He's not coming back, father," he said. "Why would he? He got what he wanted!"

Still looking at the road, his father replied in a sorrowful manner, "You still have much to learn about the ways of our God, my son." He turned and looked at him. "You are my firstborn, but if you are to lead this family one day, you will need to know far more than what you think you know!"

Tobijah didn't answer.

Aside from the beautifully ornate amphitheater where theatrical plays were staged (which Eliel enjoyed immensely because of the wonderfully strange stories which were depicted) and a hippodrome that boasted chariot races (which happened to be taking place during his time there), there was an arena where slaves who had been taken prisoner by Rome fought. Eliel had never seen such a spectacle, and part of him was curious; watching men trying to bludgeon one another seemed popular among Gentiles. Putting his moral qualms aside, he decided to attend one day.

The arena was circular and fairly large, draped with many colorful

---

deed, to focus on our pain to the exclusion of everything else is to lack perspective and proportion—perspective, in that we don't consider what God might be trying to accomplish in our life; and proportion, because our pain is really no more weightier than that of multiplied millions of others who have suffered throughout history or are suffering now. The danger, therefore, is assuming an inflated delusional state of being, seeing absolutely no value in suffering and thus disregard eternal things as we make our pain *the* primary issue. This is a serious flaw of the *ego* and, if not addressed, will keep our natural self-centeredness firmly in charge and continue hindering our spiritual growth in the most fundamental ways.

banners all around. The seats, made of thick stone and terraced to a considerable height, were packed with people as they cheered on the gore and violence. Right from the beginning of the very first contest, people were screaming and yelling for their favorite. It was as if something had taken possession of them to become so desirous of seeing someone slaughtered to death.

Eliel just happened to sit next to a man who apparently liked betting on the participants. He would shout "encouragement" to the poor souls without any sense of irony that they were fighting to the death. They were like animals in a pit to him. Entertainment at its finest!

"Come on! Go for his thigh and cripple him," the man yelled, "and then finish him off! I've got a lot of money on you!" The match was between a short, athletic man who was very quick and a taller, bigger but slower opponent; each armed with swords.

Turning to Eliel, the man said, "You would think that the chance to fight in Rome would not just be an incentive to win and live but to be revered and worshiped. Imagine the glory!" As far as Eliel was concerned, this was sensational enough; he had never seen men fight so skillfully, being so adept with swords—attacking, defending, maneuvering. No wonder they were so good at killing. But, being slaves, they really had no choice but to kill in order to not be killed.

In a brilliant move, the short man delivered a slicing cut with his sword to the other man's midsection. Blood began spurting out. People went hysterical, sensing the end was near.

Eliel decided to leave. Part of him was captivated by the show of raw power and aggression in these men, but it turned out he really didn't want to see one actually die for his amusement.

"Not your kind of entertainment, eh?" the man said as he saw Eliel get up. "You're going to miss the best part! Don't you want to see it when it happens? What's the point of coming unless you see it when it happens?"

"I've seen enough!" He started walking away.

A huge roar went up from the crowd. "Yes! Yes!" the man screamed. "Excellent!" Eliel looked back at the arena. The shorter man had "finished off" the other man who was now lying face down, his blood pooling on the arena dirt from a deep cut to the neck which almost decapitated him. The shorter man was raising his arms in victory, blood dripping down his sword. It didn't last long at all.

Apparently, the man won his bet.

A couple of weeks went by. One day Eliel decided to go his favorite tavern. There were several of them in the city but he liked this particular one. It was located away from the main thoroughfare and hordes of people but easy enough to find.

With the exception of a few square openings in the walls, it was a dark, musty place. At night it was lit outside with a torch next to the door; inside there were large candles on the tables and a few perched on the walls. The place had a certain aura about it that, at first, made Eliel feel cautious—a sense that he would be leaving a part of himself there if he proceeded. But after his first visit, his reservations went away and he got used to the place.

Now on any given day it was filled with all sorts of personalities—locals, travelers, merchants. Eliel would hear different languages being spoken by groups of people sitting at various tables. When they spoke in a dialect that was similar to his own, Eliel heard them discussing what sounded like business deals or talks of trade or just plain grotesque or vulgar things. But most were there to get drunk. They were usually a loud, boisterous bunch whom the tavern owner had to keep in line occasionally.

Gambling was also an important pastime at the tavern. At first, Eliel didn't know the rules of the game they were playing, but one day he decided to give it a try. To their pleasure, they discovered after a few rounds that he was not very good at it; it was easy money for them. *Maybe next time I'll have better luck*, he thought. There was always next time.

But on this particular day he wasn't interested in gambling. Sitting alone at a table in the corner, watching the usual cast of characters, he was drinking the tavern's house brew, a concoction that left much to be desired; nothing like the wonderful wine his father's vineyard produced. But being the only ale they served he eventually acquired a taste for it.

During previous visits he had seen women in the place, going from patron to patron and striking up conversations. Today he noticed a woman he hadn't seen before. She was of olive-colored complexion with shoulder length hair and light green eyes. She was very attractive, wearing suggestive attire and jewelry about her neck and wrists which Eliel thought were a bit gaudy; he thought they took away from her beauty. Still, he was drawn to her. Did she remind him of someone? Was she a fantasy come to life?

She was standing behind a man, leaning over him with her hands on his shoulders as he sat at the table gambling; his winnings piled in front of him. He clearly was good at this game. The other men talked loudly as they goaded one another on, trying to distract each other. The woman looked like she was trying to whisper something in his ear but he seemed irritated and began waving her off. She stood straight, looked around the place and saw Eliel staring at her, his eyes transfixed. Smiling, she left the man and headed in his direction.

"You're not from here, are you?" she said, as she walked up to him. "I can tell you're not a merchant. And if you're visiting someone I doubt you would be in this place. So, what *is* your business here in the city? Oh...apologies...my name is Anatolia."

Eliel wasn't used to a woman being so forward. She simply by-passed the usual banter one would expect to hear among people who had just met and came straight to the point. Right away, he found her personality intriguing, and a little refreshing, but her directness gave him nowhere to hide.

"Well...uh..." He was tongue-tied.

"It's alright, dear. You don't have to answer. I'm just used to talking to people like that. I don't mean anything by it...just making conversation!" She knew how some men react if they felt challenged in some way and she didn't want a confrontation. She continued standing in front of him, smiling. "You seem out of place here!"

"What do you mean by that?"

"Look around," pointing around the place with her eyes. "Is this the kind of place you *normally* hang around?"

"Well...lately, yes."

"Mmm. And before now? You lived a very different life, yes?"

"Well, I imagine we *all* lived very different lives until we chose the one we're living now!"

Anatolia laughed playfully. "Yes, I suppose there is truth in that!" *This one has a little more going on than most,* she thought. "So, are you going to tell me your name...or at least where you're from, or do I have to guess? I *am* a pretty good guesser when it comes to where people might be from."

"My name is Eliel...Okay, go ahead." Feeling less apprehensive, he was smiling now. He wanted to see if she really was as perceptive as she was boasting to be. He also liked how she purposely stood very close to him, as if to give him a good look at her. He could smell the wonderful fragrance of myrrh on her.

"Let's see..." She took a step back and eyed him up and down. "Judging from your clothes, your accent, and your mannerisms, I would say you are from a region south of here—near the Great Sea, perhaps. Or maybe I should be more respectful to our conquerors and call it the 'Roman Sea.'"

"Very impressive! You must have come into contact with a lot of people from that region." He was actually surprised that she could place him in that general area.

"Not really, I've just learned to pay attention over the years. You never know when the little things you've noticed about people might be useful later."

"I see." Eliel wondered what other things she was "noticing" about *him*. "Are you from here?" he asked. Anatolia had been smiling the whole time, but now the smile seemed forced; Eliel got the impression that this was an uncomfortable subject for her. And indeed it was. After seeing her mother killed by pirates, Anatolia, at the age of six, was taken from her home and sold to slave traders; they, in turn, sold her to fanatical religious cultists who not only gave her a new name but began grooming her for her future work. But Anatolia was not naturally compliant when it came to certain things. So, though the circumstances which brought her to the city were beyond her control—a horrific reminder of her stolen childhood—she steadfastly refused to let go of the one thing that connected her back to that time of innocence; the name her mother lovingly gave her. Anatolia.

"No...but it's my home now." Immediately, the other smile returned and she became intentional again. "I have a good feel for people. You're not like most men I've met. You don't seem to be a hopeless gambler and you're not drinking yourself into oblivion, at least not at the moment. So...are you waiting for something or *someone* interesting to come along?"

Her subtlety didn't go unnoticed. Her appeal hit its mark and she saw an all to familiar passion set ablaze. By now Eliel knew why women were in the tavern and what *their* business was, so there was no need to ask or entice her to play the seductress. But what he didn't know was that she, along with other women who worked the taverns in the city, were devotees of the goddesses, the consort of the principle god of the region. And just as the women in the goddess's temple pleasured worshipers of both genders who took part in the obligatory rituals, so it was Anatolia's duty to pleasure the tavern clientele as part of her worship.

Albeit, despite her allegiance, Anatolia was immensely unhappy. She detested *everyone* and she loathed the goddess, for the life she had "chosen" (though she never thought of it as such) had brought much sorrow and ugliness, and now she was little more than a disposable commodity in religious garb, and an easily replaceable apparatus for a vindictive deity. But this was her life, such as it was, and she knew her only real choice was to make the best of it.

Still smiling, Anatolia took her right hand and rubbed it gently against Eliel's left cheek. "You know, you are *very* handsome! I know somewhere we can go if you like. You might find what I have to show you very interesting!" Her demeanor was disarming, her words inviting. "Come!" She turned and walked towards the door, looking back briefly to see if he was following. He wasn't. She stopped. When she said, "come," Eliel saw something in that split second that gave him hesitation—a ravenous look in her eyes that said he was about to become prey to someone other than her. "Is something wrong?" she said. Eliel didn't respond. Anatolia came back to the table. "Don't be afraid, dear. I'll take good care of you." He continued sitting there looking at her. She assumed he was nervous, so she sat down across from him and placed her hand on his, hoping to put him at ease. "It's okay. We can talk a little more if you like. I don't mind."

"I would prefer that for now," he said. They continued talking for a great while, and then left the tavern together some time later.

Another week passed. Eliel didn't notice how things were steadily changing in him—more like accelerating—and that there was a growing dependence upon the very things which were causing the changes. With each encounter, something insidious seemed to deposit more of itself within him, burrowing deeper into his being and causing him to become more separated from himself and more removed from things which once had meaning for him. His soul was being ravaged and, tragically, he had adapted. But the worst part was, he had no idea where all of this was leading.

By now, the notion that he was "looking for something" seemed ludicrous to him; he was too busy having "fun!" The attention he was getting as a foreigner was intoxicating. He was in an emotional stupor most of the time, drunk on the favors and pleasures his money bought him and others. People clung to him—some for this reason and some for that reason—feeding on him like the soulish predators they were.

But it didn't take long. A little money spent here and a little money spent there—some in the same places, some on the same people—had added up to a whole lot of money spent everywhere. It was only when his resources had practically dwindled to nothing that it finally got his attention. He couldn't continue spending money like before; what little he had left had to go to lodging and food until he could get some work. The "clingers" noticed that he was being more stingy with his money and figured it was running out. They took that as their cue and began disappearing one-by-one; the boy was no longer useful to them.[13]

Another week went by. By this time the emotional numbness was beginning to lessen, and Eliel was starting to feel the damage done inside. It was considerable. He had kept company with some very calculating and unconscionable people and, having foolishly given them access to his soul, they had done what people like them always do. *How could I have let them talk me into doing those things and going to those places?* he thought. *Was I under some kind of hypnotic influence?* That explanation would have made his actions a little more bearable, but he had to accept his own culpability in this, as well as the fact that, in some ways, he had become just like them—deceitful, arrogant, manipulative. And he *let* it all happen under the guise of being "friends" and wanting to hang out. Some friends! Most of them had such an insatiable need for ego gratification—always at Eliel's expense—that they were exhausting to just be around. Others were such ghoulish fiends that, in retrospect, Eliel was certain they must have been inhabited by demonic entities. And then there were those who were so volatile, entirely capable of and willing to hurt people if they even looked at them in the wrong way, that Eliel always felt intimidated around them. He was glad to be rid of all of them.

But now another pressing issue had arisen. He had been so caught up with himself that only now did he notice things becoming more

---

[13]Webster's defines "prodigal" as "given to extravagant expenditures; expending money or other things without necessity; exceedingly recklessly wasteful; not frugal or economical." Wasting money and resources is only the visible evidence; the real impetus for wastefulness is the expenditure of time and energy pursuing *ego*-centered goals and pleasures. In other words, we are so given over to things that our very way of living and being has become "prodigal." The Greek word used here, *asotos,* is translated from the word used in the King James Version of the same Scripture (Luke 15:13), which is "riotous." This word is used only here in the entire New Testament, and it means "dissolutely, loosely" (Mounce). "Dissolute" is defined as "loose in behavior and morals; given to vice and dissipation; wanton; lewd; debauched" (Webster's). In other words, actions, attitudes, and words are so immoral and depraved that they reveal very serious character flaws. But though we may have wasted energy and resources or engaged in immorality, if we come to see the futility of it and repent, God will forgive and restore us. Thus, our wastefulness, in a marvelous way, is useful to Him. If, however, we never see what our "prodigal living" has done to us, then our life itself has been a waste.

scarce and expensive in the city, especially food. People were talking about how difficult it was for those who worked the fields for a living; the land was becoming parched due to so little rainfall in the previous months. Having worked his father's fields, Eliel knew something about dry conditions. His family had experienced tough times as well, but had always come through. But people talked about the present conditions as if they were genuinely concerned.

The city had less people now; even some people Eliel knew were no longer around. He inquired at the tavern as to what might be happening. Apparently, a lot of people, including many foreigners, were convinced that things were going to get much worse, and they decided to leave the country before it got to that point. Even Anatolia was gone, but no one at the tavern knew for sure where she went.

There was far less activity in town—no more stage plays, no more races, no more fights in the arena. Far fewer caravans were coming through the city. The usual places Eliel frequented for entertainment and pleasure were seeing far less business; some had shut down completely. The people who were still around seemed to be moving about with purpose, focused on preparing for what was to come.

And then there were the many beggars on the streets, a lot more than was usual. Men who were no longer working the fields and couldn't stay on their landlord's property were more abundant now. Street after street, Eliel saw homeless and hungry men begging for food. Some were an absolute pathetic sight. But there were also more women on the streets begging, some with children sitting beside them or infants in their arms. The entire city seemed to be transforming into one catastrophic cauldron of human misery.

Another week passed. By now, Eliel's money was completely gone; he only had enough for one more night of lodging. He asked the innkeeper if he could stay a few more days, promising to pay him when he got some work. The man laughed; he knew there was probably no work to be found anywhere in the city. He himself was struggling to survive. Since most of the foreigners were gone his inn had practically no clientele. No matter how much Eliel pleaded with him, he wouldn't budge. "No money, no room, no exceptions!" the man insisted.

Thankfully, Eliel knew someone from the tavern, a gambling buddy —Baca by name. Baca was from an area near the Great Sea as well, but he had been living in the city for a number of years. He initially came as a merchant, hoping to make his fortune buying rare items brought in from the far east and reselling them to the rich aristocrats in the city who like adorning their homes with the unusual and exotic. But now that things had taken a turn for the worse, the rich weren't buying much. Baca's business had all but vanished.

Now to Eliel, Baca was fun to be around. He was always the life of the party because he loved to gamble, and when he was on a winning streak he was unstoppable! Unfortunately, the same was true when he was on a losing steak; he never knew when to quit when he was ahead. He was one of those for whom the feeling of winning was just as important, if not more so, than the money itself.

Baca was around Tobijah's age, so Eliel naturally gravitated towards him. He was the only one with whom Eliel felt comfortable enough, especially after a few drinks, to share details of his life, and Baca was just uninterested enough in Eliel to not be judgmental.

Eliel hadn't seen Baca at the tavern for a while, and he didn't know exactly were he lived. But, after asking around he finally found his house in a part of the city that was densely populated. He showed up at his door unannounced the day after his last night at the inn. Baca's one-room house, constructed of quarried stone, beaten clay for the floor, and large wooden beans for the ceiling, was clustered tightly with other small dwellings of the same construction. The street, really an alley, was only a few feet in width, just enough for two people coming from opposite directions to pass one another.

Eliel was hoping he could persuade him into letting him stay for a while. He banged loudly on the thick, wooden door.

"Who is it?" came a gruff response from inside.

He recognized Baca's voice. He had the right house. "Baca, it's me...Eliel!"

Baca wasn't pleased to have him at his door. "How did you find me? What do you want?"

"Are we not friends? Why do you speak to me in this way? And why won't you open...?"

"We are *not* friends!"

"We're not friends?" Eliel had to think about that for a moment. So, appealing to their "friendship" wasn't going to work. "Please, I need a place to stay and..."

"We have no room! I told you that I have a wife and two kids—just enough for us. And we don't have much food!"

"Yes, yes, I understand! But can I please stay for the night? I have no money to stay at the inn and I have nowhere else to go! If I'm not your friend, then treat me like you would a stranger. I promise that I won't take advantage of your hospitality!"

Baca said nothing for a while. He knew the tradition and importance of entertaining sojourners which, technically, Eliel was. Eliel could hear voices behind the door, one sounding like Baca's wife; they were going back and forth, but their words were muffled.

Finally the door opened. Baca looked unkempt, almost unrecognizable from their days at the tavern, and he had a scowl on his face. One of his kids, a small boy, was peeking around his leg trying to get a look at the "stranger."

"One night! That is all!" Baca said. "And all I have to eat is some meal!"

"If you hadn't gambled away our money we would have more food!" his wife said scornfully from across the room. "You never thought of me or the kids, did you?" Eliel wasn't sure if coming here was a good idea after all. He really didn't want to be an added burden.

Baca turned to his wife. "Not now, woman!" Eliel saw a dejected, sad look on his face. "Come inside."

"Thank you, thank you!" Eliel said, feeling genuine relief despite having to twist his arm. He could rest for the evening.

Come morning, however, Baca's "hospitality" was far less hospitable. He, along with people everywhere, was feeling the early effects of what would turn out to be a famine, and he didn't want another hungry mouth around to concern himself with. He practically kicked Eliel out of the house at first light.

Eliel realized he was at a distinct disadvantage. Foreigners were welcome when they spent money, not when they needed help, and *no one* was willing to help him, not even when he offered to work in exchange for food—a rather straightforward proposition he thought would clearly benefit both parties. In fact, people in general were not friendly at all anymore. Some of the same people with whom he enjoyed good times and were still around seemed especially heartless now. Everything had changed and everyone was looking only after themselves.

Eliel wondered, *How will I survive?* The thought of going back home crossed his mind. *How can I do that now? They will see what a failure I have become! And what would I go back to?* That bridge was burnt. *Maybe the bad times won't last long. Maybe all I need to do is tough it out and things will eventually get better!* Deep down he knew he was deluding himself for even considering the thought.

Not really knowing what to do or where to go after leaving Baca's house, he began meandering the dirty streets from morning till late afternoon. He felt lonely and tired, but mostly hungry. He asked everyone who passed if they could spare some food; few even acknowledged his presence.

For the next several days he scavenged for food on the streets, competing with others for the little scraps he could find here and there. Most people had stopped throwing their garbage outside their houses; they were eating everything now, and so the competition for food on the streets was fierce.

Then he remembered seeing a group of children rummaging through a small pile of rancid smelling refuse on a certain street. Maybe he could still find something edible there. He walked down the main thoroughfare and turned a corner to go down a street and almost stumbled over a man lying on his back. Another man, looking like skin and bones, was sitting next to him. He immediately yelled, "food, food!"

desperately pleading with Eliel, holding up his hands.

"I have nothing to give you!" Eliel looked at the man lying on his back. His eyes were locked, staring straight ahead, not moving, nor did the rest of his body. One arm was slightly lifted up in the air, frozen in position; he had obviously been dead for hours. He looked familiar to Eliel despite his grotesque appearance; and then he remembered. It was the man from the arena—the one who liked betting on the fights between the slaves. What had happened? He must have caught the disease that was going around. The man sitting beside him asking for food was probably his friend who didn't want to leave him. Eliel looked down the street and saw another person lying on the ground who looked like they were dead, too.

"Food, food!" the man kept yelling, grabbing Eliel's cloak to keep him from leaving. He yanked it away from the man and got out of there, forgetting about the garbage.

Fear gripped his heart as vile words pummeled his mind in a virulent barrage of condemnation: *You fool! Look what has become of you! You will die in this land! If only you had your brother's common sense!* What little will-power, strength, and energy he had was quickly draining away like a broken cistern. His mind felt numb and unresponsive, as if he were being smothered mentally; he couldn't think. For the next few hours that day he wandered aimlessly through town.

It wasn't until it began getting dark that his survival instinct finally snapped him out of it; he had to find another place to sleep for the night, preferably a safer place. He had been sleeping on the streets wherever he could—next to houses, near chicken bins, in the market —but that was becoming too dangerous. There were large packs of dogs roaming around, and they were just as hungry as the humans. It was best not to even go near them, especially when they were looking for food, which they always were. If they came across a weak or dying person or an unattended child on the street and sensed an easy meal, they could become incredibly vicious and relentless. He had to find a place away from them, and away from the two-legged predators as well.

He decided to leave the city and find somewhere to sleep on the outskirts in the wooded fields. He started walking. About half a mile away, off the main road he took to enter the town, he saw a few trees in the distance. That might be a good place. He walked toward them, hoping no one saw him go in that direction.

He picked a spot that had enough dried leaves and twigs lying around that he could hear something or someone approaching. He unrolled his sleeping mat which he had been carrying, his last possession, having lost or traded his other things for morsels of food.

He laid down and tried to sleep, but sleep eluded him; the thoughts would not stop coming. *What am I going to do?*

CHAPTER 3
Leanness of Soul

> Then he went and joined himself to a citizen of that country, and he sent him into his fields to feed swine. And he would gladly have filled his stomach with the pods that the swine ate, and no one gave him anything (Luke 15:15-16).

Their house was by no means a palatial mansion like some of the wealthy who lived in cities, but it was larger than others in the village and able to entertain many guests. While most houses were situated around the square, theirs was located on the farthest edge of the village, closer to the fields. Shaped like a rectangle with a large courtyard and cistern in the middle, the walls were made of mud-brick, and the floor consisted of flat stones. Stone pillars supported the wooden beams layered with plaster that was the roof. Multiple rooms lay around the courtyard—the father and his son slept in one room, their three servants slept in another. There was a living room for eating meals and entertaining guests, a room for preparing meals, one for their two oxen, and the last room that served as a study. On one side of the house was a garden which grew an assortment of vegetables and a small vineyard that produced a modest amount of grapes; a few fig, olive, and date trees grew close to there as well. Near the edge of the field were the enclosures for their many sheep, goats, and cows. In all, their house and property provided a very comfortable and self-sufficient existence.

It was evening. Tobijah and his father had labored all day and were now entertaining two fellow villagers, one of whom grew wheat like the father. The other visitor was Nathan, the father's closest friend; barley was his crop. They had all just finished a meal together and were now reclining comfortably as they talked.

Tobijah was strangely quiet this evening. Ordinarily, he would have been actively engaged in the topic of discussion. But tonight was different. His father noticed how quiet he was and looked over at him, concluding he was deep in thought about something. Actually, Tobijah was feeling left out. It wasn't so much the content of the conversation; he was familiar with subjects that men their age often discussed and he enjoyed talking with them as they did with him. But for some reason he felt drawn to the men themselves, in particular his father. He wasn't acting or speaking any differently than he normally did, but the *way* he was and *how* he spoke caught Tobijah's attention.

His father seemed to speak from a place within—a peaceful, secure place that Tobijah could only describe as a kind of restful confidence. He had experienced this in his father before, assuming it had to do with his many years of living. That was part of it, but now he was sensing something else.

As his father talked, an image flashed into his mind—that of his father on his knees before God in prayer and worship. He frequently saw his father "being with God," as he liked to think of it, and admired his discipline and devotion. But tonight he realized his father didn't just know *about* God, he really *knew* Him; he wasn't merely familiar with God's ways, he *trusted* God's heart towards him. He related to God as a real Person and not as some abstract concept or some unknowable ethereal presence. There was something deeply personal about all of this that Tobijah found intriguing, inspiring, and unsettling all at the same time; this was not *his* experience of God.

Nathan wanted to know about Eliel. He liked the boy and was concerned for his welfare. "Have you heard anything about your youngest since he left?" he said, looking at the father. The father simply said "no," graciously letting Nathan know by his curt response that he didn't wish say anything further about it.

The other man responded right away. "He only has *one* son now!" Tobijah looked at his father.

"No," the father said firmly, "I have *two* sons!" No one said another word about it, and that was the end of the matter.

Nathan wisely changed the subject, and their talk shifted to news about a famine ravaging another country; the father had heard of it as well. Famines had happened in that part of the world before, causing much suffering for the people and long term consequences for the land. Of course, children always suffered the most. Some, he knew, would not survive the devastation, and those who did would probably develop serious developmental issues that would affect them for life;

issues that would never have arisen were it not for lack of food. This saddened the father greatly.

Some years ago, he too faced hardship as well when hordes of pillaging locusts devoured some of his crops. The Lord, however, was merciful, and the land recovered without much long term damage. But he knew that the challenges he faced in the past were nothing in comparison to what was probably happening in that far away country. He didn't know if Eliel was there or not, but his daily supplication to God would continue: *Lord God, show mercy and restrain the hand of the Evil One; keep my son alive!*

Nathan expressed hope that something like that would not happen here as well. The other man thought God might have permitted the famine as a consequence of their evil ways. He was always ready to offer his opinion about such things.

The father was a bit more circumspect. "We live in a world that is far from how God created it," he said. "We have to expect that things like this will happen at times."

Eliel awakened to what sounded like an animal crunching its way through the underbrush. No...there were several of them. He remained motionless. Whatever they were, one was moving closer to him. He heard familiar sounding grunts...wild boars, looking for food, with what sounded like little ones. If the adults sensed danger of any kind, especially having offspring, they would surely attack and tear him to pieces. *Don't move!* One seemed to be checking him out, sniffing and slightly moving his cloak around with its snout. Eliel could feel its hot breath around his feet; his breathing was becoming rapid as he became more frightened. It was all he could do to remain still!

Thankfully, the boar seemed uninterested. After several minutes, Eliel heard them all moving away slowly. He waited until it was absolutely quiet and then peeked out from under his cloak. They had disappeared. He felt light-headed; he laid there for a moment. When he finally stood to his feet he quickly put on his cloak, rolled up his sleeping mat, and headed towards the road that led to the city.

Not a soul was present until two men appeared far down the road. As they got closer, he could see how pitiful and dirty they looked; worse than him. And they looked dangerous, like they had nothing to lose by doing whatever they needed to do to survive. One was tall and lean, the other was shorter but lean as well and limping a bit. Both were barefoot.

Eliel moved to the far side of the road, but they moved that way as well, staying right in front of him, getting closer and closer. He stopped. He was getting scared. He thought about running but knew they would probably catch him in his weakened state. He starting looking for something that he could use for a weapon, but there were only small sticks and stones lying around. The men were about thirty feet in front of him now. Too late to run. They walked right up to him. Eliel knew what was coming, and it wouldn't be a request for directions.

"Money! Now!" the tall one demanded. He pulled out a dagger and held it up to Eliel's throat.

"I don't have any," Eliel said, shaking. That didn't satisfy them.

"Then give us your mat, your cloak, and your shoes!" He quickly complied. The shorter man grabbed his mat as Eliel took off his cloak.

While Eliel was looking at him…

WHOOMP!

The taller one delivered a blow to the side of Eliel's head, knocking him down. Both men began feeling around his inner garment, looking for areas which may have been specifically stitched to hide something. They found nothing, and that made them angry enough to want to really hurt him.

"You're lucky we're feeling kind today or we'd take your tunic, too!" said the tall one. "Then you'd really be naked!" The shorter one started laughing, and then spit on Eliel. They took Eliel's shoes off as he lay on the ground, then walked away with all his belongings, mumbling to each other about something in another language.

Eliel laid there. First wild boars, now robbers. *I just woke up!* he thought. *What else is going to happen today?* He sat up; the ground looked like it was moving underneath him. The side of his head hurt. He reached up and felt a large bruise, but there was no blood. He decided he'd better leave in case they did decide to come back and take his tunic. He got up but fell back down. After a minute, he finally staggered to his feet as strength returned to his legs. He headed towards the city as fast as he could, wobbling from side to side a few times as he tried to stay upright.

The city was hardly recognizable from the thriving metropolis it had once been. Aside from those who obviously couldn't leave, you wouldn't have known that throngs of people jammed the streets just a few months ago.

He went to the market. He was so hungry, *really* hungry—such that he had never known in his life. He felt a persistent gnawing in the pit of his stomach. He was physically weak, losing energy as well as weight. Still, he was much better off than some who were slowing starving and reaching a point of no return; they had little strength to do anything.

He had no money but he still looked over the scant bits of high priced food that few but the very well off could afford. He thought he might be able to steal something unnoticed. He stopped in front of one seller who was having an intense conversation with a mother who was holding an infant in her arms. The boy was crying incessantly as they talked; then he started screaming, as if in great pain. Eliel felt sorry for the child but his screams were grating on his nerves. He knew the boy was just hungry, but his mother's pleas to the seller, hoping to find some sympathy, were falling on deaf ears. He saw an opportunity to take something while the woman was distracting him, but then noticed another man, maybe a family member of the seller, standing off to the side with a heavy looking rod in his hand. Eliel knew if he were caught he would be beaten and then locked up by the authorities. And being a foreigner, who knows how long he would be there? He decided not to risk it.

He walked over to another vendor who was selling bread. The thought of stealing came again when he saw the seller, being an older man, was alone; Eliel thought he might be able to outrun him. But then he overheard some people talking about a field where there might be something to eat, about five miles out of town. From what he could gather, one of the local farmers had desperately tried to save his crop. Most of it had been lost, and what little was left was being quickly eaten by equally desperate people. Apparently, there were also some scattered fig trees close to the field.

Eliel decided to head for the field. Even if he could steal something he knew people were taking food from others when they caught them alone, and those who resisted didn't fare well. In fact, things seemed more chaotic in the city as people did whatever they wanted; trivial matters like thievery and assault were no longer concerning to the local authorities.

As he walked down the road, coming up behind him was a family —a man, woman, and three children. They were moving at a quick pace. It looked as if they had packed their last few possessions onto a small two-wheeled cart being drawn by a donkey which the man was leading as he walked alongside, holding the bridle around its head. His family sat in the cart; his wife and their small baby sitting up front and the other two kids sitting in the back with their legs dangling off the cart. They were clearly migrating elsewhere.

Eliel yelled at them as they went past. "Where are you heading?"

"North," the man yelled back. They never slowed down but kept going. Eliel heard things were a bit better there, but it was even further away from home than this country was. With no money, he might be getting into a worse situation.

Then he began looking more closely at the barren land around him, imagining how things might have been a few months ago—lush, abundant fields producing lots of food. Now it looked like a wasteland. A strong wind came through, whirling around and then forming a mini tornado, throwing dirt in the air. Eliel had difficulty seeing and breathing. He tried to cover his eyes and nose with his tunic but it did little good. He started coughing and wheezing; his eyes were burning. And the heat...his tunic clung to his sweaty body.

Then he sensed something. Everything around him—fields without crops, trees without fruit, springs without water. The outer landscape seemed a perfect reflection of his inner landscape, as though the physical barrenness of the land was mirroring the spiritual dearth in him. He was feeling on the inside what he was seeing around him. He stopped. It was an unnerving scene, an eerie convergence of outer and inner realities in a moment of synchronicity, and somehow he knew he was meant to see this. But what did it all mean?[14]

Upon arriving at the field, he saw a few people picking over what little was left. It looked like a swarm of locusts had gone through it; coming here had been a waste of time and energy. The ache in his stomach intensified. His mind went to his family. He knew they had probably finished a meal around now. He imagined what they might have eaten—bread, legumes, olives, beans, cheese, figs. His mouth began watering.

Then, in the distance, he saw a man walking through the field and coming in his direction. He looked well fed, wearing fairly nice clothes, not dirty or ragged like most; he seemed to be surveying the land. Eliel reasoned if this was the landowner then he would know about the fig trees nearby; just a few would be enough to get his energy back after his five mile trek. The man eventually made his way near to where Eliel was.

"If you're looking for food you're too late," the man said. Eliel watched the man carefully as he bent over and picked up a handful of

---

[14]God is delighted when we enjoy His blessings, but this is not all that He intends for us. His ultimate aim is *spiritual union*—that is, becoming one with Jesus even as Jesus is with the Father (John 17:20-21). So God often allows times of dryness to rouse genuine hunger and thirst in our heart for *Him*—the Living Bread and the Living Water from heaven (John 6:48; 4:14). He is trying to expand and strengthen our spiritual roots in order to move us into a deeper relationship and understanding. But how exactly does spiritual dryness do this? By proving us and showing us our heart (Deut.8:1-8). Indeed, if we have become complacent with our life or lackadaisical in spiritual matters or disobedient to His commands, God may use times of dryness to refocus our attention and energy solely towards Him for the purpose of union. During such times He may begin addressing our deepest fears and insecurities, purifying our motives and desires, exposing false beliefs and wrong attitudes, putting ungodly and fleshly tendencies to death, healing deep emotional wounds, or dealing with doubt and unbelief. *Everything* which is not of Him and stands in the way of union with Him must be dealt with. Therefore, in the midst of such adversity we must remind ourselves that we are in the hands of a loving God who is working His purpose, and that patience and trust are needed—patience that He will perform the work in our heart, and trust that how He chooses to do things is indeed the way. The end result of all of this is a pure love for God, a heart that beats as one with His, and submission to His will in all things.

dirt to examine it. "I hope the land will recover," he said to himself but loud enough for Eliel to hear. "My family has worked it for generations. It *has* to recover. I will offer a sacrifice to the gods tomorrow. Maybe they will help me this time!"

He let the dirt drop to the ground and then looked at Eliel for a moment. His clothes were torn and grimy like others, but there was something different about the boy. Ordinarily, he wouldn't have thought twice about him, but for some reason...

"Where are *you* from?" he said.

"Judea."

"Ah, the land of the Jews—the land that flows with 'milk and honey.' You won't find much of that here!" Eliel thought, *He knows something of our history!* "You're a long ways from home. What are you doing in this part of the world?"

Eliel was far too embarrassed to even think about answering that question at this point, not to mention feeling weary that he had to.

Change the subject.

"Are there any fig trees around here?" he asked.

The man laughed. "Your optimism is impressive. Look around. Everything that grew anything has been stripped bare! Like I said, you're too late!" He saw disappointment on the boy's face.

"I'm just hungry...but I can work!" Eliel was hoping the man would take the hint. It was approaching evening and a feeling of desperation came on him. He hated the fact that circumstances had him begging, but this man was the first person who was willing to even talk this much with him. Eliel thought he might be his last hope.[15]

"These are hard times for everyone," the man said, "and it would make no sense for me to take on someone now. My land is devastated and I don't know if or when it will ever be ready to produce again. If we don't get some rain before next season I might end up like you!" The man didn't let on how incredibly frightened he really was of that

---

[15]Wuest's translation of Luke 15:15 says the boy "forced himself upon one of the citizens of that country who was unwilling to hire him and only took him after persistent entreaty."

possibility—becoming like the starving rabble who roomed the streets around the city.

Eliel decided to press his case. "Sir, I've worked on farms and in fields before, so I know what is expected. I'm not asking for money, just food and shelter in exchange for my labor. If you have anything to do, I can do it. Whatever your terms are, I will accept them. I just need to eat and have a place to stay!"

"Did you not hear what I said, boy?" *Does he think that he's special?* he thought. "In any case, if I hire you, who else might show up wanting something?"

Ah, he does *have something that I can do!* "Please...please!" Eliel clasped his hands together, shaking them back and forth.

The man saw such a hapless look on Eliel's face that he started feeling sorry for him. He thought about it, looking towards his house and then back at the boy. "Well...I also raise pigs for food and to sell at the city market. Some of them have already died because of the famine, but I still have about a hundred or so that I *have* to keep alive. You can care for them."

Swine?! Swine?! Eliel thought. *I can't do that!* He was sickened by the idea, and the look on his face showed it.

"Uh-huh," the man muttered with a slight smirk. "So...it seems that what I've heard is true. You people have somewhat of a problem with pigs!"

Eliel knew he had already crossed several lines that he never thought he would, but if he were to cross this one he will have practically denied his heritage. Mosaic Law considered swine unclean beasts—not at all suitable for sacrifice—and eating them was absolutely out of the question. If someone were to see him even around them…

"Please...sir, there must be something else that I can do. I can…"

"*That is the work!*" the man shouted angrily. His attitude changed immediately. He had been growing impatient, but now he was indignant that the boy was actually trying to negotiate with him in his woeful condition! "You said you are hungry! If you want the work, take it! If not, be on your way and off my land!"

Eliel couldn't speak. His tongue and brain felt as if they were no longer connected; the words wouldn't come. He wondered if the man was deliberately showing his contempt for his beliefs and traditions. If he knew about the prohibition regarding swine, he might also know how some Jews viewed Gentiles themselves. After all, some teachers of the Law equated Gentiles with swine, as well as dogs; both were synonymous in their minds with filthiness. It was just the way things were.

The man waited for an answer but none came. He began to walk away.

"Wait!" came a shriek.

The man stopped and turned around.

"I will do it," Eliel quietly replied, his voice barely audible. He needed this man, and the man seemed to know it. But it wasn't just for his physical survival; he needed to be with *anyone* to help ward off a sense futility that had been steadily advancing, bringing with it feelings of despair. Whether he liked it or not, he and the man were now connected to one another, and not in a good way.[16]

"Good," the man said. "Do you see those trees over there? My

---

[16]The text says he "joined himself" to a citizen of the country. The word for "joined" in the Greek is *kollao* which means to "unite closely." It's usually used in reference to a person in relation to another, but also carries the connotation of one thing clinging or sticking to another (the same word is used in I Corinthians 6:16-17 where it talks about being "joined to the Lord" as opposed to being "joined to a harlot." In Ephesians 5:31, the word is strengthened with the preposition *pros* when it refers to a man leaving his father and mother and being "joined to his wife." In every instance, what is "joined" together becomes *one*). Joining together implies a connection, a bond of some form which influences behavior and speaks to identity. Consequently, the nature of the bond is important. Bonds rooted in love are healthy and mutually nourishing because they foster genuineness, intimacy, peace, and joy. We want to be around those we love because we desire closeness with them. This type of bond causes us to speak the truth and to remain faithful and steadfast when things are difficult, even if it means having to endure much pain and suffering. In contrast, bonds which are not rooted in love tend to have fear as their underlying motivation. These bonds are actually a type of avoidance mechanism which seek to avert negative feelings usually associated with things like abuse, rejection, shame, and abandonment. Bonds which are rooted in fear prevent us from growing emotionally and spiritually, and therefore keep us at an immature level of development. In this type of bond, we tend to use one another to get what we need in order to retain some sense of security, significance, belonging, or power.

house is on the other side of them, and the field where the pig's stay is just a little further away from it. You can sleep there tonight."

"You mean with the *swine?* I have to *sleep* with the *swine?*"

The man laughed. "There's a small storage structure near the field where you can sleep. You start tomorrow." And with that, the man walked towards his house.

All sorts of distasteful thoughts and feelings were swirling around in Eliel's soul. The humiliation had now come full circle. When he left home he brought shame upon his father. He knows that. And now, having squandered everything, he was being disgraced by a Jewish symbol of Gentile impurity!

Surprisingly, he felt little anger towards the man, even if his intention was to humiliate him. God alone knew how often he projected his own personal prejudices and cultural biases on to others. It was easy to do, like second nature.[17]

He'd been standing there for several minutes, and dusk was approaching. He decided to head towards the storage structure but had trouble moving his feet; they felt as if they were encased in hardened mortar.

When he got there he looked inside. It was small, maybe only eight feet long by five feet wide in size with no door but only an opening for one; just big enough for tools and supplies. It wasn't as bad as he thought it would be. It would work. He found some straw, not nearly enough for a bedding but better than nothing.

How did it come to this? he thought. *Why is all of this happening to me?* He wanted badly to blame someone but didn't know whom to blame or what to blame them for! But he was certain that someone had failed him somewhere along the line, and now *he* was paying the price. *Or maybe,* he thought, *I just came to the wrong place at the wrong time; a victim of circumstances!* Whatever was happening, life

---

[17]Projection is taking something within us that we may be unconscious of and ascribing it to another person. The intent is self-absolution by unloading ourselves of the burden we feel but have little understanding of, and then forcing another to carry it in hopes of shaming them into owning it and carrying the psychological and emotional baggage which comes with it. Thus, we feel less burdened. Projection, a pervasive psychological device, is a deadly effective tool in fallen humanity's arsenal.

was being unfair to him![18]

He sat down on the ground and watched the sun slowly set over the mountains. It was completely quiet around him, and now he was alone with his thoughts...the last place he wanted to be. He began feeling uneasy; the hush was deafening. If only he could get away from himself, or find something to distract him from this awful silence...

They had just finished eating and were sitting outside in the courtyard, enjoying the cool breeze. Tobijah felt relaxed in the moment, enough so that he thought he would breach the subject which had not been discussed up to now. He didn't know quite how to begin, and he was always careful to be respectful, but there was no use in continuing to hide things; may as well come out and just say what he was thinking.

His father noticed the look on his face and knew the boy was preoccupied with something; he was never good at concealing his feelings or concerns about something.

"What is on your mind, son?" the father asked.

Tobijah was forthright. "Why did you give him his inheritance?" There was an uncomfortable pause. "Has he *always* been your favorite?" The father had been expecting this conversation, and now it had come. He thought carefully about how he would answer.

"Son, you know that I would never dishonor our God in such a way. Did you not also receive your inheritance...a double-portion?"

"Yes," Tobijah protested, "but I didn't leave home to throw it all away! You have always taught us to be responsible, and I'm grateful for that. But you knew the way he was. You knew how the community would see our family, our name, and you knew what this would do to

---

[18]We don't always recognize why certain people have come into our life or why particular circumstances are the way they are, but both can be catalysts for us to finally face things we have been avoiding, for they sometimes cause an unconscious need to be made known, which can lead to a conscious decision to surrender to God concerning a matter. Now we naturally resist surrendering when we can't see the reason for things, but God always does that which brings glory to Him and blessings to us. So, while a part of us may say "yes" to God and another part says "no," *faith* leads us to follow Him despite the fact that we don't always understand.

us financially! How could you justify doing such a thing?"

There was another long pause.

The father saw the pain in his eyes and heard the perplexity in his voice. His heart yearned for him. But the question was not easy to answer; there were spiritual considerations that Tobijah would be hard-pressed to understand, much less accept. Still, he had to be firm and straightforward with him, for what his son interpreted as favoritism was anything but that. Indeed, the inheritance was not the issue at all; there was something far more critical—that being, the condition of Eliel's heart before God.

That aside, what the father always suspected concerning Tobijah had now been confirmed; the condition of *his* heart was just as dire, for he was just as lost as his brother. And so, his prayers intensified: *Lord God, may You soften his heart and open his eyes that he might see!*

CHAPTER 4

Awake!

> But when he came to himself, he said, "How many of my father's hired servants have bread enough and to spare, and I perish with hunger! I will arise and go to my father, and will say to him, 'Father, I have sinned against heaven and before you, and I am no longer worthy to be called your son. Make me like one of your hired servants.'" And he arose and came to his father (Luke 15:17-20).

The sun had not yet risen over the distant mountains, but a beautiful orange glow began appearing around them, making them look magnificently statuesque as night slowly began giving way to morning. The air was crisp and there was a peaceful stillness all about that Eliel purposefully tried to soak in; he was dreading the work ahead of him.

He only slept for an hour or two—tossing and turning most of the night as he tried to stay warm. Every so often he would stare at the night sky from just inside the door opening. The stars were plentiful in this part of the world, and they made him think about one of his father's favorite Psalms: *"He counts the number of the stars: He calls them all by name."* It was the first thought he'd had of God since leaving home.

He wished he still had his cloak and mat; it was cool last night, and what little straw he found did little to ease the ache and tiredness in his body on the hard ground. No matter. They were both torn and soiled. But it wasn't just the coolness and the ground—bugs would sometimes crawl on him during the night, and they always seemed to know when he was about to doze off. Some he recognized because they liked to hang around animals, searching for droppings; they were always on a mission. But others he hadn't seen before. Just then, he felt one crawling in his straggly hair and brushed it away with his hand.

Now, as the sun rose higher, flies began to congregate around him, perfectly complimenting the insufferable odor from the pigs nearby. He sat up on the ground and began swatting at them. He was miserable. How quickly life had changed! What began as the promise of unbridled freedom had become something that he could never have imagined. Gone was the euphoric feeling of unrestrained indulgence. He realized the life he had envisioned had been nothing but a fantasy all along.

"Good, you're awake," came a voice from a short distance. He turned his body to see the man coming towards him, leading a donkey laden with empty sacks on its back behind him with a rope. "Well, get up and start feeding them! I need to go into the city for the day. I'll be back this afternoon." He looked the boy over for a moment. "By the way, what is your name?"

"Eliel."

"Eliel," the man repeated as he looked at him. He saw no need to tell the boy *his* name. He turned and walked away, and then yelled over his shoulder, "And make sure *every* pig is fed well! I need them looking healthy!"

"Wait!" Eliel shouted. "What about *my* food? I need to eat, too!"

"Then eat! There's enough for all of you!" Then, with a certain fierceness, he stopped and turned. "But feed my pigs first! Understand?" He was talking about the pods that the pigs ate. The pods, which came from Carob tress, were long and slender with sweet tasting pulp and many brown bean like seeds. They were used primarily to fatten swine, but the very poor sometimes ate them. It was now obvious to Eliel that the man had no intention of feeding him anything else.

He slowly got up, almost stumbling over as a feeling of numbness went through his legs. *What am I doing here?* The whole scene was surreal to him, as if it were happening to someone else and he was only observing some poor unfortunate soul. But it *was* happening to him.

Inside the structure were a few tools along with the feed and a large pail. He picked up the pail and plunged it into a very large wooden container sitting next to it filled with the pods. He looked at them for a moment. His stomach pains started again. *Maybe just a few wouldn't be so bad.* On the heels of that thought came a feeling of uncleanness. "No!" he said out loud. He was not going to lose himself in this squalor! *Who would I be if I started eating the swine's food?*

He walked to the field with the pail. The pigs were stirring; they knew someone was bringing food. As he approached, he felt defiled just being around them. *I never should have agreed to do this!* he thought. He started throwing the pods on the ground as far away from him as possible, making sure not to get to close to the repugnant beasts. *Don't let them touch you!* They were eating the pods as quickly as he was throwing them.

Walking back to the structure, he thought of his father and things he taught about God—things he always knew deep down were true but had only rarely experienced for himself. But now he was having serious doubts. *And where is God now?* he thought. Here he was living an odious life by anyone's standards—thinking of eating the swine's food—and God felt as faraway and unreachable to him as usual.

After making many trips, all of the pigs were finally fed. Some of the piglets were squealing and running around the field, chasing one another; they were having a great time.

He noticed a tree stump that was a little ways from the smell of the field, covered in shade from a nearby tree. He headed towards it and sat down. As soon as he did, loneliness swept over him like a wave, almost knocking him over. He felt completely cut off from everything and everyone important to him; alone in the world with no one to talk to, no one who might even understand and empathize. He wondered if his sorry plight would ever change.[19]

---

[19] As beings with free will, God allows us to choose our way. Though He may corner us until we have but one direction in which to go, or place roadblocks in our way to dissuade us from continuing down a certain path, or allow the pain our choices have brought to increase exponentially, the decision as to what we will or will not do is always ours to make. Therefore, if things are not changing in our life there is a reason, and the reason is probably due to a false belief (perhaps more than one) that is drawing energy from a negative emotion (anger, fear, shame, etc) that is more than likely connected to relational issues with God. Thus, our will is being held captive. But if God is indeed all that the Scriptures declare with respect to His nature and intentions for us, then we would be wise to come to terms with this and recognize that some troubles we face in life may not always be due to some unknown reason concerning God's will, but rather an issue of the heart that reflects our own will.

He thought of Tobijah. They often talked about their hopes and dreams when they were younger—marriage, of course, being one of them. He knew Tobijah liked a certain girl in the community ever since he and her were little kids; they seemed to be made for one another, and Tobijah was sure that he would marry her one day. It was only a matter of time before he asked father to approach the parents and begin their discussions.

Eliel also wanted to get married one day, but that all seemed highly unlikely now, like a dream from a previous life. *How can I even think about getting married? And who would want to marry me? What kind of life could I ever hope to provide for her?* A sadness came over him.

Then he thought about his father. *What would he say if he saw me now?* His father wasn't one to let his emotions eclipse his thoughts on a matter. He started replaying his father's last words to him in his head and recalling the look on his face, as if he wanted to say more but couldn't. What *would* he have said?

The commandment to "honor your father and your mother" came to his mind. *Immediately*, he felt conviction. How many times had he not esteemed, valued, and honored his father in his heart, even feeling scorn for his authority on occasions, especially when he was being disciplined?

A slight fissure opened in his soul, just enough for a trickle of more shameful remembrances to pour forth—irresponsibility, selfishness, and childishness which he wholeheartedly embraced. It all seemed unbelievably atrocious to him now. *How could I have been this way for so long? How could I have treated my father that way? Maybe God is punishing me! I deserve it after the way I've been!*[20]

---

[20]Punishment would seem to be be at odds with what Jesus was trying to convey with respect to the Father's heart in this particular story. This is not to say that God does not bring judgment upon a person or nation for their disobedience. He does (II Thess.1:3-10, Rev.20:11-15). But long before that comes, God warns us and allows us to reap the negative consequences of what we have sown with respect to our choices and actions in order to open our eyes. When it comes to His children, He not only allows them to face consequences but also brings chastisement. But the pain and suffering permitted in such cases seems less retributive or punitive and more corrective and instructive in its purpose and effect. Heb.12:5-11says this: "And you have forgotten the exhortation which speaks to you as to sons: 'My son, do not despise the *chastening* of the Lord, nor be discouraged when you are rebuked by Him; *for whom the Lord loves He chastens, and*

Just then, there was a shift inside him. Up to now, he had been looking for a way to relieve his pain, but he saw how self-serving that was; it would not be enough. No, he needed the *remedy* for his soul. He realized that, like a boat that had drifted far out to sea, he had drifted away from God long before he left home, and he knew the currents were now taking him places he didn't want to go—much darker places. He keenly felt how things had taken on a life of their own as he splurged all about town, and now he shuddered to think what could have happened if things had continued unchecked.

But for the grace of God...

Slowly, coldness began giving way to warmth, rigidness to pliability, callousness to sensitivity; he was opening up, and with it came a brief glimpse of who he *really* was. Regret began flooding his soul for things he had done and words he had spoken. But mostly, he felt shame for the person he had become.

He saw that despite his father's teachings and Godly example, he chose to believe things which were not true but provided the illusion of security, power, and control his *ego* craved. It was all a farce. Deep down he knew his life was built upon lies, and that it would all come crashing down around him at some point; he would no longer able to deny what had become manifestly obvious. That time had now come.

---

scourges every son whom He receives.' If you endure chastening, God deals with you as with sons; for what son is there whom a father does not chasten? But if you are without chastening, of which all have become partakers, then you are illegitimate and not sons. Furthermore, we have had human fathers who *corrected* us, and we paid them respect. Shall we not much more readily be in subjection to the Father of spirits and live? For they indeed for a few days chastened us as seemed best to them, but He for our profit, *that we may be partakers of His holiness.* Now no chastening seems to be joyful for the present, but painful; nevertheless, *afterward it yields the peaceable fruit of righteousness to those who have been trained by it"* (italics added). The word "chastening" is the Greek word *paideuo*, which means "to teach, educate, but also to discipline, punish" (Mounce). *Paideuo* is used thirteen times in the New Testament, but only twice does it actually refer to punishment (Luke 23:16, 22 and II Cor.6:9) and never in reference to God punishing His children. The problem is when we do experience pain as a result of God's correction, we are often quick to interpret this as punishment. If we believe that God's first response to our sin is to exact punishment, or we believe He derives pleasure by punishing us, then we are attributing to Him a characteristic that is inconsistent with His nature. But since Christ took the punishment that should have rightly come on us on His cross (I Pet.2:24), God's chastisement is meant to cause us to repent, turn from our sin, and to correct and change something in our life so that we begin obeying Him in order to come back into right relationship with Him.

He knew *he* was the reason for his pain, and that nothing would change until he was willing to obey God, face the truth about himself, and take on life as it was and not how he wanted it to be.[21]

He could feel his insides trembling. He was entering new territory, and he was terrified of what realities he might encounter. But he would not be deterred from doing what he knew had to be done. He decided to take it step-by-step, beginning with what had been revealed so far, and then ask God to help him be thorough and methodical concerning every transgression.

And God did exactly that. One-by-one, things were brought to Eliel's remembrance. In fact, so many ugly things came into his consciousness that he felt like an absolute reprobate. Sins which never seemed all that horrible to him, certainly no more horrible than the sins of others, were now being seen for what they always were—an abomination to a holy and righteous God! It pained him when he realized how nonchalant his attitude had been all these years.

For the first time, he was *seeing*, and what initially began as a trickle turned into a deluge of deplorable thoughts and actions. Just recalling the filth, wickedness, and perversion that he had engaged in almost made him sick to his stomach.

He cried out to God for His mercy and purifying power—acknowledging his sins, repenting before Him, and asking for forgiveness. He knew he wasn't entitled to anything. He was guilty and deserved to be

---

[21]Often, when the pain caused by our choices outweigh the pleasures we once enjoyed, we begin looking for the way out. Until such time, God often allows suffering to continue until the heart signals its receptiveness, and we invite Him into our inner process in a way He wasn't before. Something has made an impression upon us, and now that part of us has begun to yield to Him. We go from a dogged determination to live life on our terms (often contradicting our own better judgment and best interests) to a willingness to obey God, and this often takes place within that space of time during the *ego's* partial paralysis in the midst of suffering. In other words, the dominating influence of *ego* is taken out of the equation for the moment in order that the part of us which may truly desire to change is given a chance to respond in earnest. When we permit God to enter the dark and secret places within—places which we have kept securely locked and guarded for all of our life—we may feel naked, fearful, shameful. But these are the very places in which God desires to bring His truth to bear. Godly sorrow lays the groundwork for this (II Cor.7:9-11). And because God seeks to bring us into the fullness of His love and wholeness in Christ and not merely into a better life, His work is thorough and uncompromising in intention and application.

cast aside forever; self-condemnation had already adjudicated his case and passed sentence, and he was sure God concurred with the verdict.

But to Eliel's unbounded surprise, all he could sense was God's grace and love! He felt humbled beyond measure! Amazingly, it seemed to him that, despite his wretched condition, God was simply saying, *"Come back to Me, My son!"* It was unfathomable to him!

An hour latter, he was lying prostrate on the ground in an expression of lowliness before God, but tears of joy were streaming down his face. He sensed freedom, *real* freedom from the self-imposed bondage that years of self-centered living had brought. He rolled over onto his back and raised his hands to heaven.

When he finally got up from the ground, he was emotionally and mentally drained...but he had peace in his heart and clarity in his mind. There was a beautiful, clean feeling in his being that he had never know before. But he didn't want to get ahead of things. He knew this entire exercise before God was only the beginning of a *very* long process of transformation from a life of self-gratification to a life that truly glorified God. But he was in it for the long haul, for now he had an ally within—desire; he really *wanted* to change, and he knew God could change him.[22]

It was then that something occurred to him, seemingly out of the

---

[22]It's usual to experience a tremendous sense of relief and liberation when we finally acknowledge and trust in Him who bore our sins and iniquities. But this is only the starting point of real change. Then comes the task of working through the layers of wrong attitudes, false beliefs, emotional wounds, etc., which have kept us in such a pitiful state. Up to now, we may have balked at the suggestion that we had anything to do with where we are in life. But the fact is, we had *everything* to do with it. Sadly, few of us are willing to descend to the depths of our being to find out what is really going on inside so that lasting healing can come. As one author put it, "Why do we rarely attack a problem with a determination to get at the root of things? Do we suspect intuitively that it might be more painful to face the core problem directly than to continue enduring the obvious one? Why do we settle for a level of understanding that, whether accurate or not, gives us the good feeling that at least we're doing something about our problem, but that at the same time shifts attention away from deep parts within us?" (Larry Crabb). So long as we feel better to some degree, that is usually enough for many of us, for part of us may still not want to believe that things are really that bad. Indeed, it's far worse, and only God's intervention can change it! Therefore, we all must make the trip inward if we desire genuine transformation, for God works from the inside out.

clear blue. Of the many wonderful qualities his father possessed, his concern for all those under his care was certainly one of them, and it naturally brought good memories of him to Eliel—memories that were filled with good feelings because they were based upon actual situations which had occurred and not just vague recollections.[23]

Eliel could vividly recall times when his father's patience and understanding would dramatically change a situation—such as, when conflict would erupt between he and Tobijah, or when personal matters or work problems among the servants was causing strife, or when dealing with people or challenges in the village. His father didn't always have an answer for things, nor did he ever pretend to; he knew God would bring the answer in His time. But his faith *always* brought calm to Eliel's soul, grounding him in the moment no matter how things were.

And when it came to sin, Eliel never knew his father to be so offended or condemnatory as to reject *him*. Instead, with wisdom and compassion, his father would speak the truth and admonished him to repent and do what was right before God. Eliel took comfort in this, for he knew this applied to his father as well. By watching his father closely over the years, Eliel had learned that his own sin, as egregious as it was at times, was not his father's primary focus. Indeed, reconciliation and restoration were always uppermost in his mind, for the relationship itself was the primary issue; addressing the sin was the means to that end.

---

[23]Scripture admonishes us to remember what God has done for us (Deut.7:17-18, Ps.77:10-12, Ps.105:1-6, Ps.143:5-6), for it not only reaffirms God's compassion, faithfulness, and intentions towards us in our minds but also counters what is often more natural for us—that is, remembering mostly negative things. Because of how the mind seems to work, negative memories can, when recalled, bring up feelings and thoughts in the present—so much so that we seem to re-experience the same fear, anger, shame, etc. now as we did then. So it follows that, to the extent that we can recall the specific details of a positive memory where we believe God was with us—such as, a dramatic life-changing event, a beautiful, personal moment, a wonderful but unexpected encounter—and the specific thoughts, feelings, and impressions we had at the time, including specific details or observations we had which can help give the memory more context, we can begin to feel gratitude and appreciation as we experience the same peace, compassion, joy, etc. in the present that we did initially. Recalling a positive memory of God being with us can help us to perceive His presence and give us a stronger sense of connection with Him in the present, even in the midst of difficult circumstances.

Maybe things are not beyond repair, Eliel thought. *Maybe* I'm *not beyond repair!* He felt hope rising in him, and he began reconsidering what he had once dismissed—going home.

He knew it was close to harvest. "Maybe father might consent to treating me as a hired servant," he said to himself. His father provided for all who worked for him, and there was always plenty of food to spare. "I could receive the same care as everyone else, and prove myself again!" He knew he couldn't ask to be a regular servant, for that would mean he expected to live at the house like the three other servants; that would be presumptuous. But if his father treated him like a hired servant, that would be gracious enough.[24]

He started feeling anxious as he thought about how the encounter might go. He knew his father would immediately see through him if this were some ploy, so putting on a charade would be useless; he had no defense for his words and actions anyway. The best thing to do was to be truthful and bare his heart; he knew his father would appreciate that.[25]

Slowly, as he agonized over the pain his choices had brought his family, his resolve to do what he knew was right was strengthening. He was sure this was the right course of action, but that didn't make it any easier; he would have to make things right with his father and acknowledge his sin against him just as he had done with God. His father had always taught him that to confess one's sin before God with-

---

[24]There were categories of servants: Servants who were in good standing with the family and responsible for the domestic duties within the household; servants who worked as attendants, guards, or messengers and lived and worked on the estate; and hired servants who were tradesmen and craftsmen but also earned wages for work specifically hired for. Essentially, he is hoping to become an apprentice under a hired man in order to learn a trade and perhaps be able to pay his father back.

[25] When it comes to speaking from the heart we speak out of that which is in abundance and personifies who we really are (Matt.12:33-37). Thus, feelings, motives, and desires are often primary as our head tries to communicate what is deep inside. For some this is difficult, for they secretly dread situations that require the heart; it increases the possibility of being hurt or, if one is duplicitous, betraying real intentions. If we can recite a script or play a role, we can mitigate the possibility of exposure and stay in that relatively safe place where feelings are avoided, motives concealed, and desires unclear. But the heart *must* be engaged for spiritual growth to take place, for intellectual knowledge of spiritual truths alone is not enough; we must be willing to open ourselves up to whatever God is wanting to do in us.

out doing the same to the person sinned against would not bring true reconciliation.[26]

Then, a thought came to him, one that appeared to be his own but wasn't. *What if he is unwilling to listen to you? What if he refuses to take you back? By now, he might have decided to disown you!* That was a possibility. Things may have changed dramatically back home. Eliel was starting to doubt what he was so sure of doing just a few moments ago.

Another thought followed right behind it: *You're only considering this because you're desperate! Your repentance wasn't genuine! Your just want to feel better! You're not interested in doing what is right, but only what will get you out of this situation!* Eliel began to question if his motives were genuine. Could the idea of proving himself worthy as a hired servant be just another self-serving venture, an attempt to salvage his flailing and fragile *ego*? Perhaps this really was only about pacifying his hunger, and all of this was a cleverly concocted cover story he had invented to convince himself. He didn't know for sure.

Suddenly, all thoughts of going home vanished; it seemed an exercise in futility. Plus, he had to be realistic. After all, considering all he had done, it would be a colossal display of arrogance on his part to even show his face again back home!

Like an unwary animal lured into a snare that gave the promise of something desired, he knew his circumstances were a sick contraption

---

[26]Because we are created in the very likeness and image of God (Gen.1:26), it seems certain that our words and actions do not simply affect Him with respect to His commands but also from a relational standpoint, for to sin against one created in God's image is to sin against God as well (Matt.25:31-46, Acts 9:1-4). Thus, because God intensely desires relationship with us (Ps.27:8), it follows that He is not only touched by those things which directly affect us as individuals (Heb.4:14) but by how we treat one another. So, as we confess our sin against another and the pain we have caused them, it is equally important to confess our sin against God and acknowledge the sorrow we have brought to *His* heart. We may be unaccustomed to thinking of God in this way, but the Scriptures reveal much regarding this—such as, His *jealousy* when we give allegiance to false gods (Jos.24:19-20); His *grief* over our sins (Gen.6:5-6), His *joy* when we walk in truth (III John 4); His *displeasure* when we balk at His commands (Ex.4:14); and His *compassion* when He sees our frailties (Matt.14:14). Given these and many other Scriptures, what God may experience within His own Being in relation to us should not be dismissed, for being made in His image and likeness implies we were made specifically *for* relationship, which, in turn, implies that complete wholeness in Christ is also something for which God created us (Col.2:10).

of his own making. A traitorous, haughty part of him had willingly conspired with something deceitful and malevolent to bring about his downfall, and now he was trapped. Despair once again began to enveloped him, and the little hope he was feeling earlier began to dissipate into nothingness.[27]

He was sitting on the tree stump again, and it was feeling hard on his bottom. A change in the direction of the warm breeze was sending the odor of fresh pig droppings his way; the smell was even more sickening. The sun's position had shifted as well; the shade was gone. The heat was beating down on him.

Sitting there alone in the middle of nowhere, he stared blankly ahead into the distant horizon. It was afternoon. He didn't know if he could take another day of this.

Tobijah had just finished cleaning the stall and feeding their prized calf, and now he was standing there...looking at him. He felt drawn to him today for some reason. Something about the animal made him stop and he didn't know why. Frankly, he never had much interest in taking care of him—that was Eliel's job; he actually liked spending time around him.

But now, here he was caring for the creature. He knew his father appreciated his willingness to assume Eliel's chores, but somehow that didn't seem enough. He still felt taken for granted, as though he was only doing what was expected. Yes, feeling appreciated felt good, but he thought a more purposeful recognition of his selflessness over the

---

[27]"I am no longer worthy to be called your son." The Greek word for "worthy" is *axios*. "In classical Greek *axios* had to do with tipping or balancing the scales. When two entities are compared and found of equal weight, they are 'fitting.' Since fitness implies worth, *axios* came to mean 'worthy, deserving'" (Mounce). Paul's prayer for the Colossians was that they would "be filled with the knowledge of His (God) will in all wisdom and spiritual understanding" so that they might "walk worthy of the Lord, fully pleasing Him, being fruitful in every good work and increasing in the knowledge of God" (Col.1:9-10, parenthesis added). While knowledge can be loosely defined as possessing facts and information, understanding would be the proper interpretation and meaning of the knowledge acquired, and wisdom the application of that understanding to chart a course of action. Therefore, when wisdom dictates our behavior, there can exist a "fitting" balance and, thus, an expectation of God's will being fulfilled in our life.

years would have lessened the feeling of the rebuff.

But neither would that have cured what really ailed Tobijah, for this had less to do with recognition and more to do with the belief that value came through achievements, that worth was primarily validated through works. And now this conviction, which he was sure applied to God as well, had morphed into a malignant core malady in his soul. Acceptance *had* to be earned! How could it not? The more one did for God the more God regarded that person! The idea that God simply delighted in *him* was impossible for him to seriously consider. Oh, but how badly he *wanted* to believe it was so!

Tobijah left the stall and started walking towards the wheat field when he saw Rapha, the servant who was close friends with Eliel, coming in at the same time. Rapha was around Eliel's age, and the two often acted like siblings. During previous harvests, Tobijah sometimes noticed how they would play little tricks on one another just to get a good laugh. He could tell Eliel liked having someone to joke around with—something he himself wasn't all that inclined to do with Eliel—and now Eliel and Rapha had become genuine friends. Sometimes Tobijah felt jealous for how close they seemed to one another. But he reasoned that it was because of Eliel that things weren't that way between them.

Tobijah walked up to Rapha. "Is my father still out in the field?"

"Yes," Rapha replied, noticing a bemused look on Tobijah's face. It had been a couple of months since Eliel left, and Rapha missed him. He knew it wasn't his place to ask, but he was still curious, as were the other servants. He knew he couldn't be the same way with Tobijah as he was with Eliel, but maybe he might respond to a heart-felt question. He decided to take a chance.

"Do you miss him?" Rapha asked.

"What?"

"Your brother. Do you miss him?"

"What I miss is not having to do both his work and mine!" *How can he be so brazen as to ask such a thing?* he thought. Actually, Rapha knew more about the family than Tobijah realized, and he knew a few things about Tobijah in particular.

He misses him, Rapha thought, though his resentment came through loud and clear. "Well, *I* miss him," Rapha said.

Immediately, Tobijah felt judged, as if he were being accused of not caring enough about his own brother. He did care. But this whole episode was disgraceful and humiliating to the family. Then the words, "I miss him," hit Tobijah differently. It made him feel as though he were invisible to everyone. *Even the servants prefer my brother over me!* He became angry.

"Why are you here and not attending to your duties?" he demanded. "We begin harvesting tomorrow!"

"Your father sent me to sharpen the sickles and inspect the oxen to make sure...."

"Then get to it!" Tobijah said, with a stern look. This "servant" seemed a little to casual; he thought he would set things straight. "You seem to forget that you don't just work for my father, you work for the family, which means you also work for me!"

Rapha made obeisance and left. He wasn't surprised by Tobijah's response; he never seemed that comfortable around the servants unless it had to do with the business at hand. That was alright. Once you understood that he wasn't difficult to get along with, and you could appreciate the way he was—the one who always seemed to be striving to prove himself. *Maybe one day he will find his place in God,* Rapha thought, *and then he will find rest.*

Eliel got up from the stump and began walking towards the storage structure to enjoy what little shade it provided; it was hot and stuffy inside. When he sat down on the ground a particular memory came to mind, a time when he and his father were repairing the gate to their prized calf's stall.

His father always talked about that calf with appreciation, as if he had far more value than the eye could see; a symbol of something greater. He knew his father was saving him for a special occasion. What that was, he didn't know, but the way his father spoke of the calf made Eliel feel as though he too was a part of something special, something that had spiritual significance.

Indeed, his father's words would often take on spiritual overtones, even about mundane things; simply being with him meant Eliel had to always be ready to learn whatever lesson his father was trying to teach. At times, Eliel would not only learn a spiritual truth but something of his father's essence would delicately drop inside of him. He couldn't always articulate what he was feeling, but more often than not he would know that something real had been transferred from his father to him.

But on that particular day and occasion as they worked on the gate, the conversation had to do with knowing one's purpose. His father's words stirred something in him that day, for just as the calf would eventually fulfill its purpose, Eliel thought that maybe he too was created by God for a specific purpose. His father had always told him as much, and he wanted to believe it. At the time, he did sense something deep within him being called forth, something real and heavenly but hard to grasp and even harder to articulate, and he remembered wanting to answer the call and discover God's plan for his life.

But, alas, the allure of the world beckoned him, and its tug on his soul proved stronger as he got older. Somehow he became convinced that he was missing the really important things of life—things that seemed far more exciting and promising in terms of actual fulfillment than some spiritually ineffable and tenuous thing he once sensed on the inside and now seemed impossible to lay hold of.

Some of Eliel's friends also felt as he did, and they encouraged him to follow his natural desires and appetites just as they were doing. Their words stirred his growing dissatisfaction with things as they were, and a curiosity about life beyond their village and the nearby town. Soon, the world began to encroach upon him in ways he couldn't comprehend, and he began growing impatient. There was so much he had yet to see and do, and time was wasting!

Now Eliel saw the vanity of it all, like trying to grasp air with his hand or collecting water with a fishing net. He had been taken captive by something, and the sad consequences of his choices were proof positive that that something was clearly in charge. *What was wrong with me? How could I have been so blind?* he thought, *Why couldn't I see what was happening?* He knew the answer to that; he didn't *want* to see.[28]

It was late in the afternoon. Eliel was beginning to wonder where the pig farmer was. Coincidentally, he looked down the road which led to town and there he was returning. The donkey looked to be carrying a lot of things in the sacks on its back; he saw something sticking out of the top of one of them. Eliel's mouth began to water with anticipation. Some food—real human food!

The man walked to where Eliel and the pigs were, but said nothing. After looking them over, he seemed pleased.

"Any problems?" he asked the boy.

"No, sir."

"Good. Tomorrow we'll take some of them into the city to sell if I can. We'll also pick up more feed while we're there."

The man could see expectation in Eliel's eyes, apparently for the work he had done.

"Did you eat?"

"No, sir."

---

[28]The *ego* pursuits to which we are committed retain their appeal insofar as we refuse to consider the real issues in our soul which may be driving them—in particular, the emotional or psychological damage done to us which demonic entities enjoy taking advantage of. In reality, we give these entities the right to harass us so long as we are unrepentant and continue asserting our right to determine our own destiny, or be the sole arbiter of right and wrong, or use our power as we see fit. Thus, to "come to our senses" necessarily involves a willingness to humble ourselves and lay aside these *ego* driven values so that we might truly awaken from within. Only after this has taken place can we begin learning submission to God's will as a way of life and contentment in being a reflection of His Person through Christ. Until such time, we remain in a devilish stranglehold of our own volition, in rebellion against God and His ways. This has been humanity's dilemma for thousands of years, for Satan instilled this evil in the heart of man at the fall. Thus, a prideful inflationary way of being that has arrogantly assumed the prerogatives of the Divine reveals an unholy desire to be like God. And this, whether we realize it or not, aligns us with Satan and his ongoing rebellion against God—which is, to dethrone Him and take His place (Is.14:12-15). In doing so, just as Satan seeks to dethrone God in His majesty, so we also seek to dethrone God and cast off His authority over our personal life.

"Why not? What's wrong with the feed? Is it infested?" Eliel didn't answer. Obviously, the feed was fine; he just refused to eat any. But the man was not about to give him any of his own food. He became angry. "If you don't want to eat, then that's not my problem! I'm not here to take care of you! You mean nothing to me! Do you hear! So don't think that you have a right to expect something else! I've already done more for you than most would have ever done!" He felt the boy had manipulated his way into his life and now *he* was being made to feel guilty despite trying to "help" him!

When the man calmed down, he let out a sigh, feeling bad for letting his quick temper get the best of him—again. He wasn't a bad man, just a lonely, frightened man who realized long ago, after losing his wife and two children to disease, how unpredictable life could be and how easily things could be taken away. And now, all he wanted to do was to hold on to what little he had left—cherished memories of his family and the land of his ancestors—hoping the gods wouldn't be so cruel as to once more demand a life; this time his own, by slow starvation.

He turned towards the donkey. Reaching into one of the sacks on its side, he pulled out a good size piece of bread. He had several of them. Eliel thought they must have cost him a small fortune at the market or a substantial trade of some sort.

"Here," he said, tearing off a small piece and throwing it at the boy. Eliel grabbed it and held it against his chest to keep it from falling to the ground. "See you in the morning." The man walked off.

He didn't wait one second; it was gone in a flash! Bread never tasted so good! He thought again of all the food in his father's house, and here he was groveling once more before this stranger, having a measly piece of bread—something his father had plenty of—being thrown at him like a dog.

Right then, the matter was settled. There was no more debate. He had had enough. He was going home. He would leave at sunrise.

CHAPTER 5

The Return

> But when he was still a great way off, his father saw him and had compassion, and ran and fell on his neck and kissed him. And the son said to him, "Father, I have sinned against heaven and in your sight, and am no longer worthy to be called your son." But the father said to his servants, "Bring out the best robe and put it on him, and put a ring on his hand and sandals on his feet. And bring the fatted calf here and kill it, and let us eat and be merry; for this my son was dead and is alive again; he was lost and is found." And they began to be merry (Luke 15:20-24).

He was hungry, weak, and smelled like pigs. Wearing only his tattered filthy tunic, Eliel was a sight! But he had no thoughts of how he looked. Indeed, it meant nothing to him, for by simply leaving dignity was restored. Though he grudgingly gave in to the man's demands, the demoralizing circumstance could never cause him to forsake centuries of time-honored traditions, or abandon age old precepts rooted in the Law. Rather, it wrought a deeper appreciation and a genuine humility for both that was long overdue.

A lesson, one of many, had been learned in the far country—that being, God's ways were *not* his ways. A simple lesson, but one that often takes a person a lifetime to *really* learn. That part of Eliel that seemed so set on having its way had been dealt a decisive blow, and the battle, at least on that issue, had come to an end.

But the war was not over; more battles lay ahead. But at least he knew what the war was about now and who the real enemy was. He would no longer waste time and energy foolishly fighting against the very things he needed to be fighting for.

As he walked down the road, no one passing him could have imagined the conflict that had been raging in his soul the past few weeks. All they saw was his pathetic appearance, about which some weren't shy in conveying their thoughts and feelings. A man and woman heading towards the city came up behind him and, apparently catching wind of his strong, offensive odor, walked around him, giving him a wide berth. The woman looked back in disgust, holding her nose as if to punctuate her feelings. Another man coming in the opposite direction avoided eye contact all together, hoping the boy, looking so destitute, wouldn't ask anything of him. But Eliel wasn't looking for sympathy or help. He just wanted to get home.

He had never walked this much before without sandals, and now the soles of his feet were very sore; it didn't help that he stepped on a jagged branch a while back with his left foot. When he saw a large stone off to the right side of the road, he decided to stop for a moment to rest and examine them. There was a small, open cut on his left foot and some blisters were forming in places on both feet.

Sitting there, he thought about the last few months. Nothing about him could vindicate his decision to leave home; he had zero to show for all of his gallivanting and was now in a far worst state than when he left.

He wondered, *Will I ever make it in life on my own? Will I ever amount to anything?* With no inheritance, he figured he would always be in servitude to someone, starting with his father—that is, if he agreed to it. His mind raced into the future. *When the day comes, maybe over time Tobijah will let me work alongside him again when he sees how committed I am.* But what if Tobijah insisted that he always work *for* him? He would sell himself into slavery to another before doing that! He became distressed at the prospect, but there was really no point in thinking about that right now. He got up from the stone and trudged ahead.

The journey was already feeling longer and more arduous than when he left home, and he still had to pass through the city that would forever symbolize his *ego*-centered excursion into hedonistic folly. He wished he didn't have to. His memories of the place would never be pleasant, but always a reminder of what an irrational and shameful time this was in his life. But yet that wasn't the whole story, for the city would also be remembered as the place where God mercifully began a work in him in the midst of debauchery and degradation, a work that would form the foundation for a new life. Ah, yes...a new life! Where had he heard that before?

Oh, the mysteriously wonderful ways of God!

As he came up on the city he was hoping that no one he knew would see him in his miserable state. He wanted nothing to do with any of them, but to move as quickly through the place as his tired body would allow. A thought came to him: *Will my father ever love me again?* He might agree to hire him but would he ever actually *love* him? Yes, he knew the kind of man his father was, but...he still struggled to believe. *When he finds out about all of the things that I did here...*

Eliel's heart began to sink and his pace slowed, as if to give his mind more time to think about what he was doing—whether going home was really the right thing. *Maybe*, he thought, *I should spend the rest of my life, however short it may be, here in this city!* No, he knew he had to go home. If for no other reason, he had to ask his father's forgiveness, even if meant nothing to him, even if he refused to employ him as a hired servant, and even if he were no longer welcome in the village. He smiled, seeing the irony of it all. He couldn't wait to leave home, and now he was coming back to his father; back to God the Father.[29]

Entering town, he saw only a few sellers still hawking their food at outrageous prices. There were far less people around; nothing like it used to be. He passed by the inn where he stayed; it looked deserted. He wondered if the town would ever recover, if it would ever return to the hustle and bustle for which it was known, the reason why he came in the first place. It probably would, once the rains returned and the famine subsided. Human nature being what it is, most people would simply pick up where they left off.

---

[29]When we finally see how naked, poor, and pitiful we have always been, surrender to God becomes the only logical choice, and through our humility and His grace we begin to believe that we can become the person He created us to be. Granted, we can't see all God intends, but we can see enough to permanently reject the paltry offerings of this world and the myopic life we have been living. Yet, this is a perilous moment for those who, in their littleness, are able to dilute the awesomeness of this revelation and somehow continue advancing their own pettiness, not realizing that now, having seen what God has always had in mind, they are without excuse. Conversely, the person who humbles himself understands that Christ is demanding that they lay down everything once and for all and follow Him to their death so that their life might flow effortlessly into His life—the lesser into the Greater.

He kept walking.

Now, several hours outside of town, his walk had slowed considerably. He felt listless, and the ache in his stomach wouldn't let up. He felt his midsection, then his sides; he could feel his ribs and count each one. He recalled seeing someone in town who looked like a skeleton. He knew he wasn't that far gone, but he was much thinner.

Then, far off in the distance on the left side of the road, he saw what looked like fields of grain on an elevated parcel of land. He could only make out a few people there, but they didn't appear to be workers; they looked like they were stripping off grain and eating it. *There is food there!* he thought.

As he got closer he began to run in spite of his painful feet; he was anxious to get there as fast as he could before it was all gone. He passed a trough filled with water that was near the edge of the field. *And there's water here!* When he got there he saw there wasn't much grain left, and these few people were eating as fast as they could.

He quickly began stripping grain and eating. Some of the women who saw him coming had already begun stuffing grain in small pouches they had made with their garments. He tried to do the same with his tunic but it wouldn't hold much. The race was now on to see who would get the last little bit.

But then, seeing how desperate the women were, looking far worse than himself—emaciated bodies, gaunt faces—he backed off and let them eat the rest. He still had several days to go before reaching home, and he thought the conditions would probably be better the closer he got.

After eating only a little, he was surprisingly satisfied, more so in his soul than his body. The short respite felt like a sign that God had not abandoned him, that God was with him, that God was helping him. And indeed God was, and it made Eliel feel content in the moment.

He walked over to where the trough was just outside the field, coupled his hands together, plunged them into the water, and put it to his mouth to drink. After he had his fill, he splashed some over his head. Then, forming a small cup with his right hand, he rubbed his left foot, doing the same with his left hand and right foot.

He sat on the trough for a while. "Thank you, Lord God!" he said softly. Yes, the Lord was on his mind a great deal more these days.

The wheat harvest was in full swing, and the father, Tobijah, servants, and hired hands were in the thick of it. Sickles were swinging, wheat was being tied together, and bundles were being loaded onto four-wheeled wagons harnessed to the oxen that took them to a stone threshing floor. There, servants were beating the grain with sticks in order to separate it from the straw. Others, using winnowing forks, were tossing the straw and grain up into the afternoon wind to separate them. Then, using wooden shovels, the grain was put into sieves to sift out any dirt or small stones. Lastly, servants were storing the grain in clay jars which were loaded onto wagons and carried to a large storage structure near their home.

The wheat harvest was usually the most strenuous of the year and required the most people—more so than the grape, fig, and olive harvests which wouldn't take place for another three to four months. And because the wheat harvest ushered in the Feast of Weeks, the father always offered the first fruits to God in gratitude for His bountifulness. Also, in keeping with the Law, he made sure to leave a corner portion of his field unharvested so that the poor and the sojourner could glean from it.

Tobijah stopped for a moment to wipe the sweat from his brow. His back was a little sore from all the bending needed to cut the stalks so near the ground, and his arm was tired from swinging so much, but he was thinking how good it felt to work hard. He looked around to see the progress they were making; they would be at it for a few more days.

His father was still working hard just a few feet away from him. His vigor was such that, despite his age, he could easily keep up with the younger men, sometimes putting them to shame when he kept going while they took a breather for a few moments.

Tobijah looked over at him. When his father saw him taking a break he looked at him and smiled. Tobijah felt something...honor. He felt honored to be his son, blessed to have a father like him, and proud to know that most in the community looked up to him. Sure, some still shunned him and would probably continue doing so for a while. He understood.

"Father, you don't have to be out here with us. Might it be better for you to just supervise everything this year?" He knew his father would never do that; he wanted to work with everyone else as long as he was physically able. Rapha, the servant who was close friends with Eliel, was working nearby. He could hear the conversation.

His father stood straight. "No, son. I want to be here. Besides, everyone knows their job." Then he added, "You are my right hand, my strength, my beloved son. I have always been able to depend on you to do what is needed. And I want you to know that I love you dearly."

Tobijah had heard these words before, but this time they seemed to penetrate a little deeper, resonating in his soul, as if his father recognized something in him that made him deserving of them. *Maybe he is beginning to see me in a different light!* he thought.

Being the more responsible one, the more sensible one, the more practical one, and the oldest one, Tobijah expected his father to lean on him more so than on his brother. While Eliel was never slack concerning his duties, Tobijah knew his brother didn't have the same drive and grit as he did; he was simply the baby of the family, the one who received the lion's share of attention from his father—at least that's how it seemed to Tobijah. But now that he wasn't around, Tobijah had his father all to himself, and it felt good to him.

"I love you, too, father," was his reply.

Then the father looked at the distant road heading out of the village, the same road Eliel took when he left. Tobijah knew he was still hoping against hope. Why? He couldn't understand. As far as he was concerned, that chapter in both their lives was closed, and it was time to move on. But he had stopped saying anything about it a long time ago; his words never seemed to be welcomed.

Looking at his father, his previous feelings vanished, and the words spoken just moments before seemed to lose their significance. He shook his head and went back to work. Rapha saw the change on To-bijah's face.

After walking for a few days, another night was quickly approaching. Despite the pain and weariness, he had made good progress and was hoping to arrive home sometime tomorrow afternoon. Physically, Eliel was exhausted, emotionally, he was feeling some trepidation; he was getting close.

By now the scenery had changed. There were more trees with fruit, more beautiful foliage; the drought hadn't made it this far. He could see rain clouds slowly forming in the distance. It didn't normally rain this time of year, but if rain was coming he knew it would probably be here soon and that he needed to be as far away from the road as possible; flash flooding was not unusual in these parts. Indeed, just a few hours of torrential rain could easily turn the dusty road into a muddy river.

Eliel looked at his legs and then at his feet; another blister had formed on one of them. But he didn't concern himself with that; he needed a place to sleep for the night.

A ways off from the road he saw some thick brush and trees. He walked there and found a fallen, hollowed out tree which looked like a good choice; he could fit some of his body underneath it. He looked around and saw many large leaves from a nearby tree. As he was grabbing some, he saw a fig tree a short distance away. After making his bedding he went to see if it had any figs on it; there were a few, and some on the ground. He collected them, headed back to the fallen tree, and sat down to eat.

The sky was dark and cloudy now. He settled in and tried to sleep. Within minutes the rain began as a light sprinkling, but then turned into a very heavy downpour as several cloud cells passed through the area. Earlier, he had found a short piece of half-rounded bark from a tree. He grabbed it, covered each end of the bark using his hands, and collected some rain water in it to drink.

The rain lasted a couple of hours; sleep was out of the question. But after it stopped, fatigue overtook him and, despite being wet and cold, he finally dozed off, curled up in a fetal position under the tree. He didn't feel or hear anything for the rest of the night.

Morning came as a few rays of bright sunlight streamed through the trees. A ray hit Eliel, and he opened his eyes, feeling the warmth of it on that portion of his face. He wanted to sleep a little more but he knew he had to get going if he wanted to be home by afternoon. He staggered to his feet and began walking towards the road.

Just as he expected—mud, lots of it. He tried walking parallel to the road in the open field next to it, but there were lots of thorny little plants hidden among other plants, and they were like tiny needles stabbing his already swollen feet. *Just take the road!* Mud began caking on his feet, making them look as if he were working in a brick kiln—minus the straw. Lifting each leg now required more effort to just keep moving; lift one leg, try not to fall down, then lift the other. There were so much mud that he had to go at a snail's pace. But after a few hours of walking, the road was not as sloppy a mess as before, and the mud on his feet was beginning to dry.

He pushed on.

It was afternoon. Standing on the edge of his field that was near the main road which led into town, the father was counting the number of jars that were filled with wheat. A few servants were loading more onto the wagon to take to the structure where other jars were already stored. It was a good year, and now the harvest was winding down. There was still a portion of wheat that was being cut by Tobijah and the hired servants on the far side of the field that was the furthest away from the main road and not visible from it.

Nathan, the father's close friend, had already harvested his barley field weeks earlier and had come to see how things were going. He was always impressed by how efficiently his friend was able to harvest so much land. They were standing and talking with one another as the jars of wheat were being loaded.

"How much of it do you plan to sell?" Nathan asked.

"Oh, the usual amount to the usual people in town, as well as some families here in the village. I will have more than enough left over this year for my family and everyone working for me. God has been good to me."

"To all of us," Nathan added.

"Let's go to my house. I'll draw some water for us to drink. I need to take an accounting, too." He had scribbled some figures on a parchment for his records.

As they turned to go to the house, the father looked towards the main road. He stopped. Nathan, seeing he had stopped, turned and looked as well. There, in the far distance, was a person going towards the village. The person wasn't carrying anything so they couldn't be passing through the area. Maybe they wanted some food; he had plenty so he was ready to give them some.

As the person got closer, the father saw their physical frame— scrawny and haggard looking; they were just shuffling along as they walked. Even from where he was, he could see the person looked pretty bad from head to toe. And they were naked, wearing only a tunic with no outer garment and no shoes. Maybe this was a slave looking to sell himself for food and shelter. The person's face was dark, covered with dirt or mud, their hair thoroughly soiled and matted. It was hard to make out who it was.

But as the person reached the edge of the field, the father squinted his eyes and leaned forward. His jaw slowly opened. His heart began to race. He lost his breath. His mind screamed: *IT'S HIM!*

Without saying a word, he dropped the parchment and grabbed his cloak, holding it in his hands so that he could run as fast as he could through the harvested portion of their field towards the road. Nathan thought he had gone insane, not to mention acting quite undignified for a man of his age and stature.

"What are you doing?" Nathan yelled.

The servants had just finished loading the jars when they saw the father running towards the road. "What's going on?" Rapha said. He was standing with them, not knowing what to make of this either. Then he saw the person on the road. "Who is that?...wait a minute..." Rapha couldn't believe it.

Before his father had reached him, Eliel had fallen to the ground on his knees, his last little bit of strength and will power had gotten him home, and he was spent. His father rushed towards him, knelt down, and hugged him tight, kissing him over and over. Dirt and mud were all over his face as well, but he couldn't stop. Tears were streaming down; he couldn't speak. Neither could Eliel. He wanted to hug his father back, but felt to ashamed; he wouldn't even look him in the eye. Nathan and the servants were all looking in stunned silence.[30]

After several minutes, the father very slowly lifted Eliel to his feet, holding him close. For the first time in months, they both stood face to face again. Eliel tried to clear his dry and sore throat. His lips were cracked with dried blood on them. It was hard for him to speak, but he began with the words he had rehearsed, his sincere attempt at transparency. He could see his father was happy, but he felt nothing but contrition.

Still unwilling to look into his eyes, he began. "Father..." His eyes welled up. Haltingly, he continued. "I have sinned...against heaven and in your sight..." The words sounded so empty now. Facing his father finally brought home the gravity of it all. "I'm...I'm not worthy to be called your son..."[31]

---

[30]The word in the Greek for "kissed," *kataphileo*, indicates that he kisses his son repeatedly and "with earnest gesture." He lavishes kisses upon him with great affection. And what of his compassion? The Greek word *splanchnizomai* further amplifies the meaning. It "carries the idea of being moved in the inner parts of the body...having 'visceral' feelings...true compassion can affect us in the pit of our stomachs" (Mounce). The father's entire being resonates with the joyous intensity of the moment.

[31]Having properly interpreted the meaning of an experience and integrated this new understanding into its present consciousness, *ego* is far more ready to depend upon God, but not as a passive onlooker. Though God seeks to put our independent ways of being which oppose Him to death, He does not want passivity, but rather submission. Passivity implies inactivity on our part or waiting for something to move us. Submission implies active participation with God and obedience to Him in wiling cooperation. When he first left home his attitude was "*give* me my inheritance." Now, his attitude is "*make* me a servant"—more humility and more conscious awareness of the need for compliance. When our attitude becomes "make me" instead of "give me," we are expressing

His father wouldn't let him finish before he motioned with his hand for him to stop talking. He sensed the beautiful aroma of humility, tenderheartedness, and openness that were not there before; a genuine Godly brokenness about the boy, and that was enough.

He turned and signaled for his servants who were still watching; Rapha and the other two came running. When they came to a stop they just stared at Eliel. It was really him!

"You," the father said, pointing to one and speaking softly, "prepare a warm bath for my son and care for his wounds." Then he whispered something into the servant's ear that Eliel couldn't hear.

"Yes, my lord." The servant turned and left.

"You," looking at another, "let everyone in the village know that my son has come back, and that I'm inviting them to come and rejoice with me over dinner this evening!"

"At once, my lord." He left immediately to spread the news.

To Rapha he said, "prepare the fatted calf," as he looked at Eliel, holding his head in his hands. "We will all feast tonight!" Eliel looked at his father with disbelief. Rapha grinned from ear to ear as he looked at his downtrodden friend.

"It is done, my lord," he said, and took off running.[32]

The father turned to be beside Eliel, and then, with his arm around him, urged him to walk with him towards the path that led to the village. By then, Nathan had walked towards the road and was standing at the edge of the field. He was *very* happy to see the boy, though he wondered if he ever would. As father and son walked to the village, he said, "Welcome home, son!"

Eliel managed a weak smile.

---

our desire to submit our will to God's will, wanting only what He desires for us. Contrary to what some may think, submission to God's will in no way undermines or cancels our individual uniqueness. Indeed, only when we are free from the tyranny of self can we appreciate how submission to God brings *true* freedom.

[32] The *fatted calf* here is a symbol of exuberant jubilation. Usually fed grain and kept in stalls for special celebrations, calves of this sort were large enough to conceivably feed upwards of two hundred people. In other words, this would be a banquet.

CHAPTER 6

Father Love

> Now his older son was in the field. And as he came and drew near to the house, he heard music and dancing. So he called one of the servants and asked what these things meant. And he said to him, "Your brother has come, and because he has received him safe and sound, your father has killed the fatted calf." But he was angry and would not go in. Therefore his father came out and pleaded with him. So he answered and said to his father, "Lo, these many years I have been serving you; I never transgressed your commandment at any time; and yet you never gave me a young goat, that I might make merry with my friends. But as soon as this son of yours came, who has devoured your livelihood with harlots, you killed the fatted calf for him." And he said to him, "Son, you are always with me, and all that I have is yours. It was right that we should make merry and be glad, for your brother was dead and is alive again and was lost and is found" (Luke 15:25-32).

Many came with anticipation, some out of curiosity—their wives, children, and a few servants with them. Since everyone in the village knew what had happened, they were delighted to know the boy had come home and felt honored to have been invited to such a momentous occasion. They could only imagine how incredibly agonizing it must have been for the father; only Nathan his close friend knew first-hand of his struggles.

Some were hoping to know what happened to the boy while he was gone, and maybe hear some juicy details that they could talk more about with others later. Some were concerned about community standards and cultural traditions and wanted to know how the boy planned to make restitution to his father. But, not surprisingly, a few in the village refused to come at all; they simply couldn't accept how the father handled things in the beginning, much less that he had received the boy back. Cherished family customs had been ignored, and it was all to much to overlook. His stature as a village elder and leader had greatly diminished in their mind.

But by sunset their large house was filled. Seating arrangements had been made outside in their small courtyard for all who came and many torches were lit to illuminate the gathering. Musicians were playing recognizable melodies as the people enjoyed the wine and the abundance of delicious food—particularly, the exquisitely prepared fatted calf. Everyone was having a wonderful time as they ate and socialized. The father was so pleased with the turnout.[33]

He was sitting at the head table looking out at all of the guests. Eliel was sitting by his side, looking very different from when he first arrived—clean and shaven and dressed well. But he found it hard to smile, even when people came up to greet him from time to time. Their warm hugs and kind words were obviously sincere, but he felt undeserving of their gestures. In fact, some were so gracious that they acted as if he had never left, and that this gathering was simply a community event organized for fellowship. Part of him wanted to leave, but how could he do that? His father was doing this for *him*; he set the tone for the evening. The best Eliel could do was to not let his uneasiness show too much.

After most of the guests had finished eating, the father stood and motioned to the musicians to stop playing for a moment. They did, and the place became quiet as all eyes turned to him. Eliel continued sitting, looking straight ahead at all of the guests.

"I am grateful," the father said, holding back tears, "to the God of our fathers—the God of Abraham, Isaac, and Jacob—that all of you have taken the time to be here and celebrate this very special occasion with me, the importance of which cannot be overstated!" He paused for a moment. "As you know, my son left home a few months ago. I know that many of you were concerned and others greatly troubled by the events of that day." Eliel looked down.

He continued. "But that is all behind us now. He has come home, and *that* is what matters!" Then he looked straight into the eyes of many of them, as if to underscore his words. "My son was indeed dead, but look," pointing his hand towards him, "he is *alive!* Yes, he

---

[33]The Greek word for "music" in the text is *sumphonias,* from which the English word *symphony* is derived. More than likely, musicians, and perhaps dancers, were hired for this special event.

was lost, but not anymore; he was found by our God!"[34]

Many in the audience smiled and nodded their heads. An elderly matriarch who was well respected in the village, shouted, "Blessed be the name of the Lord!"

The father smiled. "There is much more that I could say, but I want to do something which words cannot express, something which will clearly demonstrate my thoughts and feelings in this moment." Everyone looked on with great interest. What exactly was he planning to do?

The father looked over to a servant who had just walked in and was standing off to the father's left. Promptly, the servant came, holding the father's very best robe, his sandals, and his ring. The robe was beautifully tailored. When Eliel saw it, he thought, *Maybe he is going to put his robe and sandals on now. But why did he wait to do it here?*

"Stand, my son." Slowly, he got up from his seat. The father took his robe and put it on Eliel. Some in the audience gasped. The same elderly woman who shouted now clapped her hands vigorously for a few seconds; no one joined her in clapping.

Then the servant handed him the sandals. The father got down on one knee, took Eliel's sandals off and put his own sandals on his feet. He stood up.

The servant handed the father his ring. "Give me your hand, son," he said. The father placed it on the first finger of Eliel's right hand. He was speechless; he wanted to protest what his father was doing, that he was unworthy. *Why is he doing this?*[35]

----

[34]Notice that he didn't say his son was dead to him, which would have revealed his feelings about the boy, but that the boy himself was dead, which revealed his son's spiritual state. In Scripture, death also implies separation. For example, *spiritual death* is when one is separated from God because the sin nature inherited from Adam remains in them (Rom.5:12). They have not been born again (John 3:3) and are therefore separated from the life of God (Eph.2:11-13). *Physical death* is the separation of the spirit and soul from the body at the cessation of our physical, natural life (Luke 23:46). And *Eternal death* is everlasting separation from God in hell and, ultimately, the lake of fire (Rev.20:14-15; 21:8). This is the final judgment for those who have rejected Christ's offer of salvation and the forgiveness of their sins through faith in His shed blood on the cross (Matt.10:28, Rom.3:21-26).

[35]The *robe* was probably long and made of fine linen. Scribes themselves may have worn robes of this kind as they may have served to designate their rank. Referred to as

But before he could do or say anything, his father turned towards the audience and, with his arms outstretched towards heaven, offered a short prayer: "Oh, Lord God of our fathers, You have shown much grace and mercy towards Your servant, in that You have brought his son home! And now, Lord God, I beseech You, continue to watch over Your servant's son, and lead him into the paths of righteousness for Your name's sake, that he might love and serve You all the days of his life, and become the man You have ordained him to be! I humbly ask these things in Your name. Amen!"

This time, the same elderly woman in the audience shouted, "The Lord is good, and His mercy endures forever!" She clearly understood why the father was doing this.

As soon as his father had finished his prayer, Eliel heard the faint whisper of a voice deep within his heart that, despite being very gentle, came with such authority and clarity that he couldn't deny the source or misinterpret the meaning. The voice simply said, *"This is from Me!"* He began sobbing uncontrollably.[36]

---

the "best robe," it was more than likely only given to honored guests. The boy is being given the same respect. He is an honored son, and if the *father* honors him there is no higher honor. His filthy old clothes, which symbolize his old way of life, have been put off by virtue of his humility and change of heart. Spiritually, being clothed with the robe symbolizes him becoming a new person who, through repentance, has been brought into a completely new life and standing with his father and before God. *Sandals* were not normally worn by slaves, but by those who were fortunate enough to afford them. By giving his son *his* sandals, this is a clear indication that he is not receiving him back as a servant but as his beloved son. Spiritually, sandals are symbolic of walking in this new life and relationship with his father and God. The *ring* may have been one of the father's signet rings, possibly bearing an engraved mark used on official documents. It represents power and authority, perhaps bearing some similarities in that regard with the ring given by Pharaoh to Joseph (Gen.41:42-43). If so, it means the boy can now act in his father's stead concerning legal issues. Spiritually, it symbolizes exercising God's authority and resources in matters pertaining to His Kingdom.

[36]Nothing so confounds our thinking, so disarms our defenses, so confuses our strategies, so offends our sensibilities, so exposes our darkness, so opposes our fallen nature, or so captivates our soul than the love of God! God's love, being the *only* thing which can transform the heart, makes the drive for self-worth and personal power irrelevant. Indeed, the will to power is only present when Love is absent, and when Love has taken the ascendancy there is no will to power. When Love has captured our heart, we know that it is here to stay, and that there is no need to create false conditions in order to keep it. This is not to say that we can now do whatever we please in contradiction to God's Word, for to do so would violate the very essence of Love itself; giving and receiving Love means doing only what Love commands. When we love Him who *is* Love, we are free to become all that Love has created us to be. Consequently, the power of Love can-

The father turned and hugged Eliel in front of everyone, and this time Eliel hugged him back with all the strength he could muster, burying his head in his chest as he continued weeping. He felt so overcome with emotion that he thought he would collapse; his father held him tight.

Everyone present understood what the father's actions and words were meant to express to the boy, and that this was a moment he would not soon forget. They had never witnessed such a show of forgiveness and compassion. Some were crying. Others were thinking, *Would I have done this for my son after he did such a thing?* In that moment, the father was even more highly regarded in their minds.

A few, however, were alarmed. Allowing him to come back home was one thing, but this…they were murmuring to those sitting or standing next to them about what they were seeing. This was clearly unacceptable.

Then the father clapped his hands. Immediately, a company of dancers ran towards the front between the head table and the audience and began entertaining the guests with an expressive and emotional interpretation of the last few months. Through movement, music, and imagination, they told the story of the father and his son in such a dramatic way that many were in awe of the greatness and mercy of God.

But after the dancers finished some of the guests themselves wanted to express the jubilant enthusiasm they were feeling by dancing as well. Chairs and tables were hurriedly moved aside to make room as

---

not be overstated, for it shapes our character, forms our beliefs, and grounds our being. Yet, some of us are unwilling to admit our need for Love; others are terrified of opening their heart to Love and giving themselves over to it because of the inherent vulnerability it brings and the possibility of being hurt; and then there are those of us who are unwilling to allow Love to completely take over, for we intuitively know it will unmask every false thing in us while, at the same time, demand everything from us. So, we often test Love to see if it can indeed deal with the darkness within, not retreating in horror or disgust but penetrating the deepest levels of our being and restoring us to wholeness. And seeing that it can, we are more inclined to embrace it. We also discover how dramatically it affects every relationship we have, for Love in its pure essence can descend into the very heart of darkness within another and not be tainted by it in the least. Indeed, Love can go places where nothing else can, changing everything in its path no matter the state of corruption. Some of us may still vehemently protest the importance of Love in our life, but it seems that Love, despite what we may have experienced in the past with regards to it, may be far more important to our emotional and psychological well-being than we realize.

the musicians began playing, and the once hallowed atmosphere became festive as beautiful music filled the air. People were not only dancing but singing—the women in a circle among themselves, and the men in a circle among themselves. A feeling of joyous abandonment broke out among them. It became contagious, as if the holy angels themselves had joined in the celebration!

Father and son joined in the dance, their arms around one another as Eliel, singing and smiling, danced gingerly in spite his sore feet; he wasn't about to let his discomfort spoil the joy and love he was feeling!

He stole a brief glance of his father. In that moment, he felt connected to him in a way he hadn't before. He sensed a newfound confidence of who he was to his father and what he meant to him. That connection and confidence would eventually find its deepest fulfillment in God Himself, for a new foundation had been laid; he was entering a new place in God where parts of him could slowly begin to heal and be put together as they were intended. He couldn't have explained what this place was if he tried, nor could he have shown others how to get there. All he knew was that he simply made a decision to follow what he always knew to be true deep inside, and that he was no longer where he used to be. It felt absolutely wonderful! In time, he would learn to *live* from this new place, from his center where God lived; and he would find his purpose in life.

As it turned out, he *had* been looking for something, and in the midst of the most improbable of circumstances, he found it, or rather, was found by the One whom his heart was longing for but didn't realize it. From this point on, God was no longer his father's God; God was now *his* God.

It had been a long day, and Tobijah was coming in from the field. The harvest was finally over and he was looking forward to a time of relaxation. He and his father always enjoyed being with one another after a hard day's work, and Tobijah thought it might be a good time to speak with him about his role around the estate. *After all*, he thought, *the time will come for father to scale back his involvement in things and let me assume more responsibility.* He was hoping his father would lay out a clear plan for the inevitable transfer of responsibilities.

It was dark now, and from the part of the field which was close to the village Tobijah could see more light than was normal emanating from it. When he got to the square he saw many torches aflame...and he heard the sound of music, the kind that was normally played at merry occasions. But what could the occasion be, especially on such short notice? *Did the community receive good news of some kind? Is someone important paying the village a visit?*

Then he realized all the activity was coming from *his* house. His father personally knew people who held high positions of authority in the region; perhaps one was passing through and decided to honor father with his presence.

As he approached their house, the servants, as well as servants from other houses in the village, were standing outside talking. Why were *they* here? *It* must *be someone important,* he thought, *and father needed more help for the evening!*

He walked up to the servants. Rapha, Eliel's close friend, was among them. Tobijah directed his question to him.

"Who important has arrived?" he asked excitedly.

They began looking at one another with concern; obviously no one told him. Rapha knew this could potentially be a very explosive encounter. He was always respectful, but he really wanted to be careful and sensitive; he was aware of Tobijah's feelings about his brother. It would probably be best to not say anything about the ceremony.

"Uh...your brother has come back home...and your father invited everyone to come and celebrate his return." He studied Tobijah's face. "He killed the fatted calf for him."

To the servants, Tobijah looked like he was thinking about the statement, as though his mind was trying to understand what he had just heard. Actually, he was in a kind of daze, as if he had been hit with something over the head and was just starting to come around again.

But as they stood and watched, they saw something come over Tobijah; his countenance changed. Rapha didn't like what he was seeing and started getting nervous. He had never known Tobijah to be violent, but since he was the messenger he thought it best to leave before he got blamed for something.

"If you would, please excuse your servants," he said, "we must get back to the celebration and attend to the guests." Rapha made a quick bow and turned and left to go inside the house, not waiting for a response; the others followed right behind him.

The music was still playing, people were still dancing, laughter and conversations were still coming from the house. Tobijah just stood there.

He had the audacity to come back home? And my father is "celebrating" his return?

It was inconceivable to him! He thought about how faithfully he had served his father—for years! Now, like some old worn out tool that had served its purpose, he was being discarded. He felt deeply hurt, used, and betrayed. His loyalty, obedience, and hard work obviously meant nothing![37]

---

[37]Dependable and committed, he has a clear sense of what he believes constitutes right and wrong. For him, what is right is upholding family traditions and established roles in society which give one grounding and continuity; what is wrong is to dismiss these cultural norms in pursuit of irrational desires and personal pleasures. What is right is honoring and obeying your elders; what is wrong is disgracing your father by besmirching his name. What is right is remaining faithful to what has given you identity and purpose; what is wrong is showing contempt for this by rejecting what has made you who you are. Yet, despite his convictions, he is a lonely soul—the forgotten one whose pain has now become unbearable. Spiritually, he symbolizes some today whose life is more painful than joyful, more dutiful than experiential, more robotic than responsive, and more religious than relational. He is like those who labor faithfully for God, going through their entire lives sensing little that would suggest He takes pleasure in them. They often wonder what is missing, what they are doing wrong, or what more God requires of them. They are hurting badly, but they have learned to live with it, along with the disappointment of a life that feels woefully unfulfilled. This is their normal Christian experience, the best they believe it will ever get this side of Heaven, and most anything else would feel very abnormal to them. But it is a potentially dangerous place to be in, especially for extended times, for we can very easily decide that life with God has not measured up to what we have been taught, and now we begin looking for significance, acceptance, and fulfillment elsewhere. Usually this is very subtle at first, but over time as the things of the world provide the immediate relief that we seek, we go deeper and deeper, not realizing that our heart is no longer as it once was before God, and that our love for the world has taken precedence over our love for Him (I John 2:15-17). We have departed from God, and now the world has our heart.

He recalled his father's words to him during harvest—words that, at the time, gave him reason to hope that things would be different between them, that his frustration around their relationship would soon be a thing of the past. The words felt meaningless now.

Then a thought occurred to him: *And why didn't father send someone to tell me that my brother was home?* He was getting angrier by the minute as old festering wounds in his soul were inflamed anew. In that moment, he knew he could say or do anything and feel absolutely no remorse. And that fact didn't bother him one bit; he had a right to feel this way!

Just then, Nathan, his father's closest friend, came out of the house and stood just outside the door. He was looking up at the brightly lit full moon in the night sky, thinking about the ceremony for the boy and marveling at his friend's compassion. When he looked slightly to his right, he saw someone standing about a stone's throw away from the house, silhouetted by the torches against the dark night. He realized it was Tobijah.

"Oh, there you are," he said, walking over to where he was. "People have been wondering where you are."

"Have they, now?"

Nathan hesitated for a moment, trying to formulate his next words. "Son, I don't know what you're feeling in this moment, but will you not at least go inside? Knowing your father as I do, it would mean a great deal to him!"

"And why would I do that? For him to further humiliate me?"

"Humiliate you?" Nathan was taken back by his response. If he were his father he would have been thoroughly insulted! He was about to give him a short lecture but sensed it would be pointless. He shook his head and, with a very sad look, said, "You know a great deal about farming because of your father, and his estate will be in good hands when you take over. Of this I'm sure. But..." Feeling pity, he added, "it's painfully clear you've learned little else from him!" He turned and walked towards the house. *So,* he thought, *you have chosen to make this about you—how it makes* you *feel, how it makes* you *look! How tragic!*

Tobijah immediately shot back: "You're mistaken! I've learned who is valued in this family and who is expendable!" Nathan never looked back but kept walking until he disappeared into the house. Tobijah was seething.

The father saw his friend come through the door and walked over to him. "Have you seen my oldest?" Nathan had to take a moment to compose himself. He was disturbed, and the father noticed it and wondered why.

"He's outside," he said. "He refuses to come in."

The father took a deep breath and sighed, looking down at the floor. He headed for the door. Tobijah heard the door open and turned to see his father. For a few seconds, they both just looked at one another. In that moment, they could not have been more emotionally and spiritually distant. Regardless, this was an astonishing day, and his son needed to know the incredible significance of it and what it all meant —not just to him as a father but for the family! He walked to where Tobijah was.

"Son, you have always made your thoughts and feelings clear to me about this matter. I understand how you have felt. And I can only imagine how you might feel right now. I know this is not easy. But for this evening, I am asking you to put all of that aside. Your brother has returned home. There will come a time when we will all talk. But for now, *please* come inside and see him."[38]

Tobijah could take no more. Years of pent up frustration, anger, and sibling jealousy were about to come together into one titanic explosion. Shaking his finger at him in a degrading manner, it was clear to the father that his son had lost much respect for him. He looked into Tobijah's eyes and saw an intensity he had never seen before. He readied himself.

---

[38]In the Greek, the word "pleaded" is *parakaleo*, which means "to ask, implore, summons" (Mounce). This is not what one would normally expect to see from paternal authority at the time. Further, when the father addresses him as "son," he uses the Greek word *teknon*, a general term for "child," stressing the fact that he is dear to him. Jesus used this word when describing his love and desire for Jerusalem (Matt.23:37). It's clear that this is a tender attempt to reach the angry little boy he has been for some time. And this seems to confound him even more, for as angry as he is, he still needs his father to *be a father* to him in this moment, and his father does exactly that.

"First, you give him his inheritance, knowing he would squander every last bit of it! And now, after wasting your livelihood with whores and who knows on what other foolishness, you honor him for simply coming home? You have violated cultural traditions and made a mockery of our family! He may have dishonored you in the beginning by his scandalous behavior, but you have disgraced yourself!"

His father said nothing.

"Am I not your *firstborn*? Have I not done *everything* you have asked of me? Have I not kept *all* of your commandments?" The father was about to respond that he had indeed obeyed him in all things, but the question was rhetorical; Tobijah wasn't interested in an answer.

By now, the sound of Tobijah's voice had caught the attention of a few servants who happened to be standing near the door inside the house. Opening it slightly, they couldn't believe what they were hearing. One servant giggled nervously. Others looked at one another in shock. One put his hand over his mouth, feeling shame for even listening to such a lurid display of disrespect for one's father.

They shut the door.

"All my life I have tried to be the man I thought I needed to be, the kind of man that the Law says I needed to be...someone you would be proud of! But all you have ever done in return is to throw me meager scraps here and there, apparently just to appease me! I have been faithful to you, and yet, for all this, you never thought once to honor me among my friends—not even with a young goat! But now, this son of yours...*him* you have honored before the whole community...by killing our prized fatted calf!"[39]

---

[39]Goats played an important role on the "Day of Atonement"—a national day of contrition and confession of sin which the Jewish people observed once a year. The observance went like this: First, the high priest made a sacrifice for his own sins by offering a bull. He then took the blood from the bull, entered the most holy place in the temple and sprinkled its blood on the front of and before the mercy seat which was above the Ark of the Covenant, thus assuring he was properly cleansed to mediate the sins of the people. Then, two male goats were chosen as a sin offering for the people. One was slaughtered and its blood sprinkled within the most holy place as well. The high priest then brought the other live goat, placed his hands on its head, and confessed over it all the sins of the people, thereby symbolically transferring their sins onto the goat. The goat was then sent into the wilderness and released. Thus, the term, "scapegoat," or literally, "goat of removal." While the boy's specific reference to a goat implies that he

The pain of his entire life, a life he now believed was fruitless, had finally come into clear focus. Still, the father said nothing but continued looking at him.

With tears beginning to moisten his eyes, he finally found the words his heart had been searching for. The tone of his voice was softer, his words breaking a bit.

"You say that I have made my thoughts and feelings clear about all of this. Well...so have you. It's clear to me now...he is far more dear to you than I will ever be!"

Silence.

For what seemed like an eternity, neither one said anything. The sound of leaves being rustled about by a gentle breeze blowing them across the ground was now slightly audible over the noise inside the house, as was the chorus of a few crickets in the distance; an uncomfortably strange calm after such a volatile tirade.

Any other father might have been furious with him, perhaps beating him severely as punishment for his insolence. But a deep sense of compassion began to stir within his heart, taking him by surprise; not that he had no compassion for his son but because it seemed especially overpowering to him in the moment, as though it didn't originate from him.

Tobijah continued to stare his father down, watery eyes and all, just waiting for him to say something argumentative that would give him a reason to keep going; his father wouldn't take the bait. He moved closer to his son so that they were now only a few feet apart. His speech was calm.

"Son, I know you are hurting terribly, not just because I gave your brother his inheritance but because of my decision to receive him back. And I understand. My heart hurts for you. But I want you to

---

believes his father thinks so little of him that even a goat is more than he deserves, it may also suggest that he sees himself as the scapegoat of the family; all positive qualities have been attributed to his brother, while all negative qualities have been transferred onto him. Indeed, the act of honoring his brother has made him feel completely separated from the family. And the fact that he was not told of his brother's return could easily be interpreted that he has been sent away into a "social wilderness" with respect to family relations.

know that I love you dearly and..."

"But obviously not as much as you love him!" he defiantly interrupted. "Do you have that little regard for me that you think your words can now pacify me when I have seen the proof of your 'love' with my own eyes?"

"What I did for your brother *had* to be done."

"What? Why?" He couldn't believe what he was hearing!

"Your brother was dead—even *before* he left home, he was dead. Do you understand? But now he is alive because something *in* him has come alive. He was lost...just as you are right now." Tobijah didn't appreciate that. "But God found him and brought him home! Do you not see how this could have ended in tragedy for your brother if things had been different? I would be remiss to not celebrate his return, and to acknowledge the new life I see in him and its promise of spiritual fruit!" Tobijah looked down, shook his head and wiped his face.

"Look at me, son." He did. "It's very important that you, his only brother, *be* a brother to him at this critical time in his life. You should know that he is not the same as he was when he left." Tobijah was hearing the words, but he wasn't buying them.

"You have always been with me, and for this I am thankful, for I have always been able to depend upon you. But this is what I hope you will realize and appreciate. You possess qualities that your brother doesn't have, qualities which have made you who you are today. But Eliel now has qualities that *you* don't have, qualities which are just as needful if you are to one day lead this family in a way that truly honors God. So, I could never favor one of you over the other!"

What "qualities" does my brother supposedly possess now? Tobijah thought. *What could they possibly be?*

Despite his father's words, Tobijah could not—no, *would* not—welcome Eliel back home, much less believe that he was "not the same" person. Whatever his father was talking about, he was being naive at best. He *wanted* to see this so-called "change" for an excuse to let him come back. *He hasn't changed!* he thought. *This is all a ruse because*

he realizes he made a huge mistake, and now he must face the conse-
quences! He wanted to live as vagabond, so let him continue to be one
somewhere else!

But the father knew there was another matter of importance—that being, the inheritance. He would address it now.

"Because your brother has already spent his inheritance, there is nothing more that I can give to him. I will continue to manage things and receive the profits, but everything I have is yours. I know you will be wise and diligent in handling all of the resources that will eventually come under your care. I only ask that, when that day comes, you remember that he is your *brother...* your *only* brother, and to treat him as you would want to be treated if the circumstances were reversed." Tobijah just looked at him.

He put his right hand on Tobijah's left shoulder and said, "Come, let us go inside." Tobijah shrugged his shoulder away; he wasn't going anywhere. The divide between them was now unbridgeable—a yawning chasm—and Tobijah saw no need to pretend otherwise. In that moment, something in him went cold; his heart turned away from his father, and his father sensed it immediately.

What the servants witnessed earlier was just the initial sign of a mild implosion in Tobijah; his father felt the full detonation. But after years of misinterpreting words and actions, it was inevitable that opposing forces within the boy would violently collide with one another. And now that they had, his father could see the extent of the deception. Something had amassed a hideous amount of power over Tobijah, and he had clearly given a part of himself over to it. [40]

---

[40]The degree to which something has power over us is determined, to a large extent, by our beliefs and choices. If our beliefs and choices are rooted in God's truth, we give the Holy Spirit the access He needs to continue changing our heart. If, however, our beliefs and choices oppose what is true and based upon Scripture, the enemy of our soul has the upper hand, and he will deceive us into enslaving ourselves, and the bars around us will be every bit as confining as any outer restraints, for we end up playing the roles of inmate, guard, and warden as a collective psychological ensemble. We become self-absorbed, rigid, and unable to meet others on a level other than our own; static in our way of being. Admittedly, there is comfort and familiarity in this, for through our interpretive grid we usually find the meaning and structure that perfectly suits our *ego*-centered outlook. But this comes with a price, for what is genuine, factual, or true is often rejected in favor of maintaining our present point of view. This is a terrible price to pay

The father was grieved. There was no doubt that Tobijah was dedicated to God as he understood Him, and that his knowledge of the
Law was impressive. But there were times when his zeal would form
an almost impenetrable shell of intolerance about him that masquer-
aded as piety. The father had hoped, through his own imperfect example, that Tobijah would have rejected the trappings that tainted the
faith of their people—even among some of their religious leaders—
and instead, follow the Spirit of the Law in which it was given.

Lamentably, that was not the case.[41]

The father realized that he was now in a similar position with his
oldest as he once was with his youngest, and that this would be yet
another test, among many in his life, of his faith in God.

____

and, in the end, is not worth it, for at some point the emotional turbulence which in-
evitably comes with this trade off spills over into other areas, making true life in the
spirit impossible. Usually, this doesn't become apparent until the deeper resources from
our interior are needed to deal with something difficult, and there is no answer, for by
this time we may have become so one-sided that we now have little access to and little
resources within our inner world. And because our energy and focus have been devoted
primarily to *ego* pursuits instead of our relationship with God, our ability to perceive
Him through the light of conscience is greatly impaired because of our constant habit of
ignoring it.

[41]The apostle Paul told the Galatian believers that the Law was "our tutor to bring us to
Christ, that we might be justified by faith. But after faith has come, we are no longer
under a tutor" (Gal.3:24-25). It seems to be the propensity for we humans to completely
overlook how laws, which are usually only taken in external ways, also speak to us
about our nature, for the primary reason that laws are necessary to regulate behavior is
because of our inability or unwillingness self-regulate. Jesus was even more specific:
"You have heard that it was said to those of old, 'You shall not murder, and whoever
murders will be in danger of the judgment.' But I say to you that whoever is angry with
his brother without a cause shall be in danger of the judgment" (Matt.5:21-22). Anger
can sometimes lead to violence, and violence can sometimes tragically lead to murder.
So while the Law of Moses dealt primarily with exterior behavior, Jesus deals with the
heart, the real impetus for our behavior. Therefore, if the heart is *not* devoted to Christ,
this is clearly demonstrated by how we live our life. If the heart *is* devoted to Christ,
this too is clearly demonstrated by how we live our life. In other words, what we do
outwardly is a reflection of who we are inwardly. It all begins with what is in the heart
(Mk.7:20-23).

CHAPTER 7

A Religious Man

It was early morning when they set out. Jars full of wheat had been loaded onto the four-wheeled wagon and tied down firmly by Eliel and Rapha, and now father and son were heading to the nearby town to do business. The oxen pulling the cart were moving at a slow, steady pace down the dusty, bumpy road, and they hoped to arrive at their destination within twenty minutes.

The father was confident of selling all of his wheat to his usual buyers in town—resellers, bakeries, and individuals who bought for their families. He had been selling his crop there for many years, and the people faithfully waited for him because they knew they could buy at a good price.

He especially wanted Eliel to come with him on this trip. Eliel felt blessed to be with his father or, more accurately, that his father wanted to be with him. And he could tell it wasn't due to some sense of parental duty. It made him feel prized and cherished. It wasn't an entirely new feeling, but for some reason the meaning of it had finally sunk in. *He really wants to be with me!* he thought.

The time passed quickly as they went down the road, the conversation varying from how the harvest went to how others in the village fared this year. Eliel was thinking how good he felt as they strengthened their bond with one another; and not only this, but what his father did for him the previous evening. He could still feel the wonder, radiance, and humbleness that the ceremony left in his soul. He would always be able to feel it.

But he was expecting their conversation to shift to expectations or inquiries—his father's conditions for his continued stay or questions regarding his travels. It never did. Out of guilt, Eliel almost felt compelled to bring things up himself and talk about what he did while he was gone. He didn't think it would change his father's decision to take him back, but he thought his father needed to know. He just wanted to be honest with him.

But as they rode on, he reasoned if his father was really interested he would have already brought up the topic. Perhaps it was better to just follow his lead and talk about it if and when he wanted to. In the meantime, he continued soaking up the good feeling of just being with him again. He had to admit, it was reaching something deep within him that needed it!

They were sitting side by side as his father handled the reins on the oxen. After a few moments of silence, his father cleared his throat to speak.

"Son, I imagine you have many questions and concerns, and with the Lord's help we will address all of them in the days and weeks to come. For now, you need to know two things: you are loved and valued, for you are and will always be cherished of God. Never doubt this! You are my beloved son, but do not think that you are my favorite, for though my love for you and your brother may be expressed differently at times, it is the same." Eliel understood what his father was saying and smiled. "Having said that, never think that you are so important that everything must revolve around you! *God* must become your source, your center, your very reason for being, and submission to His will must become your natural way of life. Hear what I say to you, son!"

"Yes, father." Indeed, Eliel *was* hearing his words and listening very intently, more so than ever.

"The Lord God gave you a small glimpse into your heart, and it has rightly humbled you and put His fear within you! And because of this, He has been able to plow fallow ground and plant precious seed, the fruit of which will serve you well throughout your life. I urge you to not judge yourself to harshly, for God has always seen the many stones and thorns of your life, even as you have always been under His loving, watchful eyes!"

Eliel kind of knew what his father was talking about; something did feel uprooted inside, and something else—holy, awe inspiring—felt like it had settled in its place. But since that night, unruly and ungodly thoughts assailed him. He couldn't comprehend all that was going on, but he knew he didn't want to do anything that might jeopardize its growth; he was finally moving towards God, and his was grateful.

The wagon bounced around as it went over some small ditches. "*This* is what we will build upon," his father said looking at him, "the seeds which God has planted within you. Many of the things I taught you growing up will now have much greater meaning because of what God has done, and those areas in your life which have been sorely wanting will be addressed in His time." He paused and looked at him. "I trust you are ready to fully obey Him in all things."[42]

"Yes, father," is all he could say. His father's words and the look on his face let Eliel know it was time for him to do serious business with God. He knew he had a long way to go, but he was willing to listen, learn, and obey. He was following a well trodden path blazed by his father and others who had gone before him, and it would lead to real meaning, to an undisturbed peace, to a fervent passion, and maybe to a deep sense of knowing God the way his father did.

They were silent again as they neared the town, his father looking straight ahead as if in contemplation or communion. Eliel looked over at him and smiled. Despite his experiences in the far country, he felt safe in the world again; his father had made it so by simply being who he was. He felt *very* grateful to have such a father, and for the first time, he didn't just respect him. He really wanted to be like him.

With the wheat harvest finished for the year, Tobijah turned his attention towards their livestock—sheep, goats, and cattle. First, he

---

[42]Jesus once said, "Not everyone who says to Me, 'Lord, Lord,' shall enter the kingdom of heaven, but he who does the will of My father in heaven. Many will say to Me in that day, 'Lord, Lord, have we not prophesied in Your name, cast out demons in Your name, and done many wonders in Your name?' And then I will declare to them, 'I never knew you; depart from Me, you who practice lawlessness!'" (Matt.7:21-23). The context of this Scripture has to do with false prophets (Matt.7:15), but it applies to any follower of Christ. To call Jesus "Lord" (Greek: *kyrios*) is to acknowledge His Supremacy over all creation, but to confess that He is *your* Lord means you acknowledge Him as your Master. The word "master" refers to one who rules, having absolute control, authority, power, and dominion. It not only seems to imply respect but an understanding that the one who is known as such is worthy in and of themselves. To claim Jesus as your "Lord" means He is *your Master* and that your are *His servant*. Paul understood this when he called himself "a bondservant (Greek:*doulos*-slave) of Jesus Christ" (Rom.1:1). As a "slave," Paul willingly placed himself under Christ's authority because he recognized Jesus' inherent right to such authority over him. As a result, Jesus had the "mastery" over Paul's heart and life (Acts 9:3-6).

would lead the sheep to graze in a familiar pasture that was not far from the village, then he would see to the goats. Usually, one of the servants shepherded the sheep but today he wanted to do it; being with the sheep would give him time to be alone for much of the day to think about things.

He was disappointed that father had chosen to take Eliel instead of him. Going to town with the harvest was important to him; it gave him the opportunity to meet more of the people his father knew and to handle many of the transactions himself. People recognized that he was a person of integrity and fairness just as his father, so they were just as comfortable doing business with him as they were with his father.

With his staff in one hand and his sling in the other, he walked from the house towards the sheep-fold. It was a rectangular-shaped enclosure protected by stone walls about four feet high with thorn bushes growing all the way around and reaching to the top of the wall. He and his father had built the enclosure many years ago as they began acquiring more sheep, far more than could stay in one of the rooms in the house. Together, they also built the enclosures for their many goats and their small herd of cattle.

The sheep started moving towards the gate when they saw Tobijah approaching. He opened it. "Come on!" They all began following.

After about a ten minute walk they arrived in the pasture and the sheep began eating. He went over to a huge rock that the servants usually sat upon to watch over them as they grazed. From there he could look in all directions to see if a predator was approaching.

Immediately, his thoughts turned to the "celebration" the previous night. *What was it father said? Oh, that it was "right" that we should "make merry and be glad." Well, if my brother was "lost," it was because of his choices!*

Since that night, he felt his world had been turned upside down. Nothing seemed to make sense any more. He had questions, and the more he thought about things, the more questions he had. *How could such a thing go unpunished? How could someone bring such reproach upon a family and then come home to a party?* He wondered what was the point of living righteously. Why be upright in word and deed if anything goes and nothing matters?

Eliel's return had changed everything. *Why couldn't he have just stayed away? Things were different. I was beginning to feel closer to father!* Tobijah felt bad for having the thought, but that *was* how he felt. He thought if only he could have kept Eliel on the reprehensible side of the moral ledger instead of now having to relate to this so-called "new person" that this would have made things a lot easier, not to mention a lot less confusing. He thought he was being forced into something that was not only unfair but putting undue pressure on him.[43]

Actually, Tobijah was more frightened than angry. This whole situation was challenging everything he knew about his father—and about God. How should he see his father now? How should he see God now? And where did *he* fit into this new paradigm? He felt a tenacious compulsion to hang on to what he believed to be right, especially since his father no longer seemed to know—his judgment being so clouded by the matter—lest the very foundation beneath him disintegrate into nothingness.

His thoughts turned to the Law.

I don't understand. Father taught us that God is gracious and forgiving...but he also taught us that He is righteous. Does this not mean He must judge His people for their sins? How is this any different from someone who ignores His commands? Moses' words came to his mind: *'Cursed is the one who treats his father or his mother with con-*

---

[43]Growing up is never easy, and this is especially true when you're already grown! When, as adults, we persist in seeing things through the lens of our childhood, growth—mental, emotional, spiritual—becomes nearly impossible, for the "child parts" within us often refuse the demands of growth. There could be many reasons for this, but the bottom line is that we do not want to change, and this is often related to issues of power or identity that are fear or anger based. The apostle Paul said this: "When I was a child, I spoke as a child, I understood as a child, I thought as a child; but when I became a man, I put away childish things" (I Cor.13:11). The words "put away" translates from the Greek word *katargeo*, which means "to reduce to inactivity" (Vine). In short, we "put away" the childish notion that growth will somehow just happen and instead assume responsibility by taking the necessary steps in order to grow. We may have had no say with respect to what happened to us as children, but we have everything to do with how we choose to respond to our pain as adults.

tempt?' Tobijah thought, *Did Eliel not do this?*

Where is God in this injustice? How can He continue to sit by during such a travesty? Has not Eliel brought shame to His holy name as well? Tobijah was building a solid case in his mind, believing he was firmly rooted in the Law and traditions which had guided his people for generations. Surely, God was on his side concerning this matter.

One of the lambs had strayed to far in search of grass more to its liking. Tobijah got down from the rock, walked over to where it was and, moving in front of it, gently prodded it back with his staff to where it needed to be. The lamb ran back to the rest of the flock. As he walked back, he sensed something on the inside, an intuitive knowing of the meaning of a thing: *"Do you see how you went after your little one when it wandered from the flock? Should I not have gone after My little one who went astray? Is he not more important than your lamb?"*

Tobijah froze.

It was late afternoon when Eliel and his father left town and began heading back to their village. It had been a good day, meeting old friends, catching up on things, purchasing needful items for the house, and selling all of their grain at a good price.

Eliel wasn't naturally disposed towards the planting and harvesting aspect of their lives, preferring instead to care for their livestock, which his father loved about him and encouraged as they spent time together getting to know each individual in their flocks and herd. But he did manage to learn a few things regarding the quality of their harvest and how to negotiate a good price. And many of the townsfolk who were accustomed to seeing Tobijah were pleasantly surprised to see him with his father.

Aside from business interactions, their conversations during the day were relaxed, engaging, even humorous at times; there was a new closeness that both were enjoying. And when it came to spiritual subjects, everything was striking a chord with Eliel, as if he were hearing his father's words again for the first time. He never realized how spiritually famished he was! His father sensed it and was careful to listen and respond to him in ways that would speak directly to his heart.

Their village was in view now, the house only a few minutes away. Both father and son had been quiet for several minutes as they rode along; the father was thanking God for the day and Eliel was reflecting on it. But Eliel was concerned about something that had not been brought up so far in their conversations.

"Father," he started, looking down at the bottom of the wagon, "he won't receive me back. He won't even look at me. I know what I did hurt him as well as you. But...I don't know how I should relate to him. We are further apart now than ever before, and it feels like things will never change between us!" He felt responsible for the way things were between him and Tobijah—the coolness that had develop between them over the years. Things which he never considered before were weighing heavy on his mind now, and he wondered what he could do in order for their relationship to be more civil.

His father looked at him. "You will indeed need to make things right with your brother, and I pray he will respond in kind. But if not, know that his thoughts and feelings on this matter are his to carry and not yours, for he has chosen to hold on to his present disposition. One day, when his eyes are fully open, he will see what God has done and what He truly values, and it will be up to him at that time to accept or reject the truth that is before him. Do you understand?"

"I think so."

"I trust our God that you will again enjoy being brothers like you were when you were young. But until then, do not allow his words or attitude to provoke you into being defensive and judgmental as he has been, nor are you to let the way he sees you to define who you now are. You are to simply love him as your brother. Will you do these things I have asked?"

"Yes, father."

Eliel knew this would be a tall order. Tobijah could be overbearing at times, especially when he was insistent about a thing, and Eliel knew his own weaknesses and tendencies and feelings of inadequacy; simply learning how to *be with* Tobijah was going to be a challenge.

But this new sense of God within him was giving him strength, and grace was giving him hope that, no matter what, he was *not* going back to that old way of thinking and being.[44]

Just as they were pulling up to their house, Eliel saw Tobijah coming back from the pasture with the sheep, heading towards their enclosure on the opposite side of their house. He could feel his body tensing up and his stomach developing knots as he anticipated their next encounter.

The father brought the wagon to a stop. "Here, take the reins," as he handed them over to Eliel. "Take the wagon to where it belongs around back, unload the jars and store them, see to the needs of the oxen for the night, and then come inside. I'm going to talk with your brother."

"Yes, father."

His father slowly stepped off the wagon, a little sore from the journey, as well as from days of harvesting, and headed towards the sheepfold. After signaling the oxen to pull, Eliel looked over at Tobijah just before the wagon disappeared around the corner of the house. Tobijah never looked his way.

Tobijah had just closed the gate behind him when he saw his father approaching. He could tell a talk was coming on, and immediately felt anxious and defensive. As far as he was concerned, there was nothing to talk about. But he knew that wouldn't stop his father.

"Is the flock well?" the father inquired. "Any sign of the wolves that

---

[44]Genuine transformation often brings a sense of being a little out of sync with the familiar surroundings and people in our life—meaning, we don't quite "fit in" that well anymore. Beliefs, desires, and thoughts have changed, and what motivated us before no longer does so. The pressure to fit in may still be coming from all around us and, perhaps, a little still from within, but we find there is far less in us that wants to conform. And if we did manage to find a way to fit in, it would probably mean forfeiting something of the new experience during the time we may still be *trying* to "fit in." Thus, the Apostle Paul's admonition to the new followers of Christ in Rome is just as applicable to us as it was to them: "Stop assuming an outward expression that does not come from within you and is not representative of what you are in your inner being but is patterned after this age. But change your outward expression to one that comes from within and is representative of your inner being by the renewing of your mind" (Rom.12:2, Wuest Translation). For our own peace and well-being, as well as for a witness to those around us of the glory and power of Christ in our life, it's best to just simply *be* who God created us to be and let others grapple with it if they must.

have been watching us the past few days?"

"No, father. They seemed to have moved on. And the flock is fine. Every individual is accounted for." Tobijah started to walk away.

"One moment, son." Tobijah stopped, still looking in the opposite direction. "Have you given any thought to what I said?"

It was all Tobijah *could* think about since that night, but not in the way his father was probably hoping. In fact, the more he thought about it the more resentful he became, for it was obvious that he was not only expected to adapt to this new arrangement but to change some aspect of himself.

He turned around. "Father, I'm well aware of my responsibilities, and I will never disappoint you in that regard. But I can't just forget all that has happened and simply go back to the way things were!"

"No, son. None of us can go back to the way things were. And it would be impossible to forget what has happened. I'm asking you to clear your conscience before God and forgive your brother."[45]

Tobijah went over it in his head: *First, he hasn't asked me to forgive him! Second, somehow my attitude is in question? And third, now I must forgive after what he did?* He was about to explode once again.

But then, that strong intuitive sense he had when he was in the sheep pasture came back to him. He looked away from his father, as if to quell the subtle pressure he was feeling. He tried to suppress it but that didn't work; he argued with it but it kept winning the debate; it

---

[45]Unforgiveness is a poison that runs through our soul and slowly kills any spiritual aspirations we may have, keeping us stagnate and stuck at that particular place in time when the offense occurred. In other words, we stop growing. Now depending upon the nature of the offense, extending forgiveness to another may be the most difficult thing we may ever do in life. But as long as we continue holding on to unforgiveness or harboring a desire for revenge, we remain bound to the person by that sin—meaning, the offender is not free from the guilt of what they have done and the offended is not free from the pain of what was done to them. Forgiveness begins as an act of the will. First, we *choose* to forgive out of obedience to God. Then, we reject and begin dismantling the specific beliefs in our heart which continue justifying our unforgiveness, replacing them with the Word of God. Lastly, we become willing to face our raw emotions so that God can begin healing our heart. But the most important thing about forgiveness is this: When we refuse to forgive others, God, in His righteousness, will not forgive us (Matt.6:14-15), thus opening the door for demonic oppression to take place (Matt.18:21-35), for how can we rightly ask God to forgive us for sins against Him when we are unwilling to forgive those who have sinned against us?

wouldn't go away. Oh, how he wished he could just make it go away!

His father stood there watching. He could see conflict in Tobijah's eyes, and his heart longed for him. But he wouldn't intervene just yet; God was *doing* something right then, God was *going after* something in him right then, and it was best to remain silent, especially since Tobijah no longer had the same respect for him. He would trust God to do what he could never do.

Tobijah continued looking at everything around him instead of his father—the house, the sheep enclosure. He was agitated. After a few moments of silence, his father spoke. "Son, come inside the house. We will all sit down together and eat, and then we will talk for as long as we need to—you, your brother, and I—and say whatever is on our hearts to one another. The Lord will be with us, and He will help us to move forward."

"I have to attend to the goats," he said angrily.

His father knew it was to late in the evening for that. "That can wait!" He saw that he needed to be more direct. "Son, the Lord is with you just as He is with your brother, and it may very well be that, because of circumstances, He has chosen this time to do something wonderful in your life!" His emotions began welling up. "I have long been troubled by the enmity between the two of you, and have agonized in prayer before our God. But I can see His hand at work in both of you in this matter!

"Your brother sees how antagonistic his posturing has always been, and he is repentant. And now, may God examine and prove *your* mind and heart, for your indignation in this matter has already become a stench in your life; it is not born out of truth and compassion but pain! And now I am sorrowful, for since you were a boy I have taught you how to walk before our God; you *know* the way of righteousness! I solemnly warn you, son, unforgiveness will eat away at your heart and defile every aspect of your life! Now our God is indeed merciful and patient, but do not force His hand, for you will be tempting the Lord in this matter. And as for me, I cannot allow this evil to gain a foothold in our home; it will bring much grief upon us all!" Tobijah knew his father *never* spoke such words lightly; he also knew he was speaking from a place of compassion, not condemnation. Still, he thought the real "stench" was Eliel's actions!

His father wasn't finished. "You know the Law well, but the *work* of the Law has yet to be written upon your heart, for you are still much consumed with yourself, and therefore unable to love God with your *whole* being!" The look on Tobijah's face was incredulous. "And now you are at a fork in the road. What you decide today will likely set you on a path that will determine your spiritual development from this point on! You *must* grasp the reality that is before you; God is offering you eternal treasure! Lay hold of Him, my son, for you may not pass this way again!" He came closer and spoke softly, putting both hands on Tobijah's shoulders. "The challenges you face are different from those of your brother. But just as I walk with him in his journey, so I walk with you in yours. I *know* of your courage and commitment, but you are in much need of God's loving care and gentle touch! Lay aside thoughts of who you *think* you should be. Let God show you *where* you truly are, let Him love you *as* you truly are, and He will graciously meet you with the Balm of Gilead for your soul! *Please...* come inside."

He turned and walked towards the house. Tobijah stood there, unsure of what to do. Deep down he loved Eliel and, though he never expressed it, hoped they could reconcile one day. But he thought that was entirely contingent upon Eliel's attitude and actions.

But what was more disconcerting was his father's assessment of his spiritual state. Part of Tobijah was moved by his impassioned plea, even though he didn't understand it all. But the more part still sought vindication; he felt unfairly judged and misunderstood. He wanted to argue his case more forcibly, point out the real issues, justify his position; show his father just how well he really did know the Law!

That nagging intuitive sense he got in the sheep pasture came back again, and the pressure was building; its deeper meaning was starting to dawn on him, urging him in a particular way. He thought it only concerned Eliel, but it was more than that.

He thought about that night. He had never spoken to his father in that way before. Granted, at the time it felt justified, even cathartic in some way, but he knew it was one thing to express his anger and another to purposely and openly shame his father. Looking back, he was relieved no one else heard it. He was beside himself!

His thoughts turned to his mother. As a boy, he remembered the sadness and disorientation he felt when she passed. His father was the solid rock he could go to, but she was the refreshing oasis he drank from, the one who never downplayed the truth or undermined his father's authority, but provided the nurturing he sometimes needed. With her characteristic gentleness and understanding, she would have addressed the internal discord he was feeling.

Oh, how he wished she was here! He was feeling strangely orphaned, and it surprised him! But he quickly surmised the reason for it. He loved his father, and knew his father loved him, but he didn't understand him anymore—his reasoning, his intentions. Yes, the time alone with him during Eliel's absence brought much blessing to the parts of his soul which still had "father-hunger," but now the relationship felt...adversarial. He was feeling alone.

This was all so confusing! He needed to sort things out, but that meant having to look at himself, and he was never one to do that; he never saw any reason to. In fact, he still hadn't processed his father's words from the previous night. To him it seemed like a veil had lifted within him that night, exposing the veneer that had been his life. The very things he always depended upon (things which actually had little to do with *genuine* faith and spiritual life) had been unmasked. And now, he took his father's latest words to mean that he was *not* who he thought he was, that something was wrong with *him*! Even his conscience seemed to be brutalizing him, casting one rebuke after another and bringing every thought and attitude into question.

Everything seemed to be hitting the same sore spot in Tobijah's beleaguered soul and delivering the same message—that he was lacking in some way and therefore failing. And indeed he was, but *not* for the reasons he thought. He couldn't see the fatal flaw that, despite his desire for genuine connection and close relationships with others, what he believed deep down about himself and the way things ought to be almost ensured that this would not likely happen. Sadly, over time, and quite unintentionally, he had isolated himself from others and made God little more than an appendage in his life.

Now no one in the village who really knew Tobijah thought he was a bad person, least of all his family. Indeed, everyone appreciated his many excellent qualities; Tobijah often sensed their unfeigned admiration for him. But somewhere along the line he had concluded that no matter what he did he could never measure up to the ideals which had become the driving forces in his life. And now that he had firmly settled into that mindset, the events of the last few days had only made him feel worse about himself.

Of course, this was only his distorted estimation of things, because the real issue was quite different. The fact was, he was at war with truth, and therefore at odds with God Himself. And as for his conscience...though it felt like a deadly enemy, it was actually a friend. A *very good* friend.[46]

Something dropped into Tobijah's heart; he felt a stirring. God was letting him know that He was with him, that He understood him, and that He would help him. Grace was present. Tobijah felt comforted, but very apprehensive; he knew it meant releasing his grip on things.[47]

---

[46]Aside from the few faults and flaws that we see and willingly acknowledge, we're often oblivious to the more fundamental maladies in our soul which are diametrically opposed to God. But when God opens our eyes we begin to see as *He* sees. Only then do we *truly* see. Until such time, we can have a very childlike outlook that is still rooted in rebellion and fantasies of our own creation, causing us to participate in a collective delusion with others, a demonic simulation where things are *never* as they appear to be.

[47]Grace, as the Apostle Paul discovered (II Cor.12:1-10), is that which reveals God's greatness and wisdom as over against our smallness and confusion. Grace is that incomprehensible, all encompassing aspect of God's nature revealed in His unmerited and undeserved favor and goodness towards us; it is God doing for us what we cannot do for ourselves. In Paul's case, grace was most apparent when he endured and triumphed over things which might have otherwise destroyed him, especially persecution. Yet, God's grace is not simply evident during these times, but also in our daily life when, to our dismay, we finally discover that we cannot change ourselves, especially when we have become wholly dependent upon certain "means" to go through life—that is, particular abilities and strategies which have proven successful over time in securing the things we seek in life. These "means" may have become so natural for us that our faith in them is obvious. And because they find their source in our core "self," we can become so self-centered that we simply can't imagine surviving without these "means." But God would not have us live this way, for our "means" are a creation of the "self" and have no basis in truth and spiritual reality as it exists. So, grace must step in and get us back on track towards God's intention for us in Christ. Like Jacob, God has to "touch" our "means" (Gen.32:22-32) so that we might see them for what they have al-

It was getting late and he still wanted to see to the goats; that would give him a good reason to not go inside right now. But he couldn't move at all; the contention in his soul was keeping him right where he was. Just as his father said he was at a critical juncture, and a decision had to be made. He didn't know it but things were hanging precariously in the balance, for he could only hold the tension of these contrary thoughts and feelings for so long before the feud between them would destroy the life that could have been, but tragically never was.

But he couldn't let it go. "I know that I'm right!" he said out loud. A nefarious, unseen entity smiled as it watched Tobijah with hateful glee. Its tireless efforts over the years had payed off, and it was rather pleased as it admired its handiwork; religiosity was still very strong in the boy, and that was good. But the entity had no intention of stopping there, especially now that it had a tactical advantage, for this was never just about the boy. There was still much work to be done if he was to become the useful tool who could one day subvert the Godly authority of the house. The smoldering embers of pride, fear, and resentment needed continual fanning to keep him moving in the right direction. Turning him away from his father that night was only the beginning; the next step would be to turn him *against* him.

Tobijah continued standing near the sheepfold for several more minutes. He was trying to plan his next move, but he was drawing a blank. *What should I do?* he thought, *What should I do?*

Slowly, in a seemingly mournful display of resignation, he began walking towards the house.

---

ways been. And after being "touched," grace, that indispensable reality of spiritual life, enables us to be, to do and to discover who we are in Christ, for apart from Him our identity largely constitutes a false self. As one author put it, "Our 'identity' is not what we take into a relationship, but what we draw out of it. It is something we do not have at all unless we discover it through reciprocity with others. The very concept of 'person' refers not to any entity in its own right, detachable and independent, but rather to a state of being that is absolutely contingent, arising out of and thoroughly dependent upon mutuality. We exist not in ourselves, but only in relation to God, and to others, and this is a truth which holds even for God Himself" (Mike Mason). Indeed, we tend to reflect back to others how we see them and who they are by the very way in which we relate to them. And so it is with God, for by the way He relates to us He is telling us who we are in relation to Him, and by the way we relate to Him we tell Him who He is to us.

About the Author

Fred M. Taylor has worked as a chaplain in hospital settings as well as a chaplain/counselor in the field of drug and alcohol rehabilitation. With degrees in psychology and Christian ministry, Fred has taught Bible college courses in spiritual life and development as well as ministering in churches and conferences abroad. His passion has always been centered on understanding God's design of the human heart and mind as it relates to having a relationship with Jesus Christ.

Dear Reader,

Thank you for reading this book! I hope you enjoyed it. But more than this, I hope you have come to see how much Jesus really loves you. He died for your sins in order that you might be reconciled to God the Father and experience the love, peace, and joy He has always wanted for you. But for that to become a reality in your life, you must make a decision to follow Christ.

It starts with being "born again" (John 3:7) and receiving a new life in Jesus (John 1:12). The Bible says "that if you confess with your mouth the Lord Jesus and believe in your heart that God has raised Him from the dead, you will be saved. For with the heart one believes unto righteousness, and with the mouth confession is made unto salvation" (Rom.10:9-10). If you would like to do this, then here is a simple prayer that you can pray. There is nothing magical in these words, and the prayer itself cannot save you. The prayer simply verbalizes your heart's desire for Jesus Christ to become your Lord and Savior and your intention to follow Him.

"God, I come to you now in the name of Your Son Jesus. I acknowledge my sins before You and humbly ask for Your forgiveness. Lord Jesus, I believe you died for my sins and rose from the dead. I turn from my former way of life and commit my life fully to You. I acknowledge You as my Lord and Savior. Fill me with your precious Holy Spirit so that I might love and serve You with all of my heart from this day forward. Thank you, Father, in Jesus name!"

If you prayed this prayer and meant it with all of your heart, welcome to the family of God! Now comes the challenging part—learning how to live this new life as you follow Jesus! First, you must understand these two truths: 1) Jesus lives inside of you now. 2) Satan hates you!

Concerning the first truth, I strongly encourage you to begin reading the New Testament, beginning with the gospel of Matthew so that you might learn about the One to whom you have given your life. Next, if you can find a church that teaches the truth of Scripture that would be great. But just as important, seek out those who are mature followers of Christ with whom you can enjoy close fellowship and receive encouragement. Being baptized in water is another thing you will want to do as soon as possible. I encourage you to talk with God daily. He is your Father now. He loves you and wants you to enjoy all that Christ did for you on the cross so that you might become all that He created you to be.

Now concerning the second truth. By acknowledging Christ as your Master, you are now in *His* service. Therefore, your life is no longer your own but about loving and obeying *Him*, even if it means giving up your life! II Timothy 2:3-4 says this: "You therefore must *endure hardship as a good soldier of Jesus Christ*. No one engaged in warfare entangles himself with the affairs of this life, that he may *please him* who enlisted him as a soldier" (italics added).

Because Satan hates the fact that you have chosen Jesus over him, he will do everything he can to destroy the new life you have and your new relationship with Jesus. Stand firm on God's promises; He will strengthen you and always be with you! As you read the Scriptures and listen to solid teaching, you will learn about your authority over the devil through Jesus and how to do use it.

By acknowledging Christ as your Lord, you have changed your eternal destiny! And so, my prayer for you is that your journey may lead you into the fullness of Christ and all He created you to be!

Shalom!